The Indians in American Society

THE INDIANS
IN
AMERICAN SOCIETY

*From the Revolutionary War
to the Present*

Francis Paul Prucha

University of California Press
Berkeley • Los Angeles • London

These essays were presented as the Thomas I. Gasson Lectures at
Boston College on November 30, 1983, March 14, 1984,
November 7, 1984, and March 13, 1985.

University of California Press
Berkeley and Los Angeles, California

University of California Press, Ltd.
London, England

Copyright © 1985 by The Regents of the University of California
First paperback printing 1988
Library of Congress Cataloging in Publication Data

Prucha, Francis Paul.
    The Indians in American society.

    Essays presented as the Gasson lectures at Boston College on
Nov. 30, 1983, Mar. 14, 1984, Nov. 7, 1984, and Mar. 13, 1985.
    Includes index.
    Contents: Paternalism—Dependency—Indian rights—[etc.]
    1. Indians of North America—Government relations—Addresses,
essays, lectures. I. Title.
E93.P9665   1985   973'.0497   85–1023
ISBN 0-520-06344-9

Printed in the United States of America

2 3 4 5 6 7 8 9

Contents

Preface

When I accepted appointment as Thomas I. Gasson Professor at Boston College for the two academic years 1983–84 and 1984–85, part of my commitment was to give a public lecture each semester on some topic related to my research interests. I agreed to the responsibility eagerly, for it provided an excellent opportunity for me to present to an educated audience—but one for whom Indian affairs were not of special concern—a brief statement on the place of Indians in American society, both in the historic past and in the ongoing present.

I had just completed work on a comprehensive history of the United States government's Indian policy, published in two volumes under the title *The Great Father: The United States Government and the American Indians* (Lincoln: University of Nebraska Press, 1984), and the Gasson Lectures gave me the incentive to distill from that large work some themes and patterns that might make sense to the nonspecialist without being completely useless to scholars in the field. The positive reception of the lectures, from a diverse audience of scholars, teachers, and students, encouraged me to prepare them for publication.

The theme of *The Great Father*, as the title implies, is the paternalistic policy that marked much of the United States government's dealings with the Indians. I have repeated that theme here but with greater emphasis on the dependency that was both the cause and the result of the paternalism.

In focusing on the many manifestations of paternalism, I of course do not intend to deny other aspects of the complex events and policies that marked American Indian affairs. There was concern for national security, for example, which dictated removal of Indians from coastal and other strategic areas. There was a need, too often augmented by avarice, for land on the part of the rapidly growing white population and a capitalistic interest in exploitation of natural resources. There was on the part of many a sense of superiority that resulted, not in benevolence, but in contempt and disdain for the Indians. Some of these motivations and attitudes were stronger among frontiersmen than they were among federal officials, who often sought to restrain the frontier whites and soften their aggressions, but they were also part of the milieu in which the government agents and the humanitarian reformers interested in the Indians worked. All this played a significant part in America's past, yet I believe that no full understanding of Indian history is possible without giving serious consideration and weight to the paternalistic spirit.

The first two essays deal with the history of Indian-white relations from the American Revolution to 1920, a period in which fundamental outlines of American Indian policy were established. The final two essays carry the story from 1920 to 1980, six decades of remarkable change in the status of the Indians. By so dividing the topic I hoped to avoid a popular error of thinking about Indians only in the romantic past and not as continuing vibrant human communities changing and adapting to the world around them.

The revival of concern for Indian rights, responsibilities, and self-determination has created inescapable tensions and paradoxes. They need to be understood and squarely faced, of course, by both the Indians and historians. Because it is difficult to appraise these current movements without the perspective that time alone brings, I offer my conclusions about them with a certain tentativeness but also with the hope that they will be informative and stimulating. The Indians, once facilely thought to be a vanishing race as a result of disappearance into the dominant white society, are instead persistent and clearly identifiable groups within the nation, whose history it behooves us all to know, and whose rights and dignity it becomes us all to respect.

Boston College   Francis Paul Prucha, S.J.

1
Paternalism

One of the enduring issues facing the government and the people of the United States through two centuries of existence is the place of American Indians in American society. Unlike other ethnic minorities that emigrated to the New World in historic times, the native Americans were in a sense indigenous. They laid claim to the land of the entire continent, which they had inhabited since their own migrations from Asia twenty-five to forty thousand years ago. By the time Europeans came to settle permanently in the New World, the Indians had developed a remarkable diversity of languages, political organizations, and other cultural patterns, but the European invaders lumped them all together as "Indians" and then devised political, economic, and often military arrangements for intercultural contacts. From 1607, the date of the first permanent English settlement in North America, to the Revolutionary War, more than a century and a half later, the American colonies and the British imperial government established procedures that formed the basis for the Indian policy of the United States. Yet responsible officials of the new nation had to adjust and adapt and create as the relations between the two races and cultures changed.

There have been numerous attempts to narrate the history of the United States government's relations with the Indians and to describe the principles of American Indian policy. It is not an easy task, for the subject is too complex to be seen accurately in black and white. The relations were increasingly anomalous, and historical patterns could not be applied automatically by the United States in its encounter with the aboriginal peoples. Nor did the Indians, on their side, have coordinated strategies for dealing with the newcomers. The outcome during the two centuries of United States national existence, however, was clear enough: Europeans and their descendants replaced the Indians on the continent, and ownership of the land was transferred from Indians to whites.

How did the officials of the American government who were responsible for Indian affairs view the relations between whites and Indians? How did they understand the plans and policies they proposed and implemented? What were the roots of American Indian policy?

Some recent attempts to answer these questions, unfortunately, tell us more about the views and commitments of the writers than about the historical reality itself. In the guilt-ridden decades of the 1960s and 1970s, we were regaled with accounts of ruthless extermination—not of whites by ferocious savage Indians, a once-popular view in the early history of American settlement, but of Indians by whites. The story was about a "conquistador mentality" that sought to eliminate the Indians physically in order to fulfill the covetous desires of the whites for Indian lands. The emphasis has been on dispossession, on a heartless disregard of the rights of Indians, and on universal treaty-breaking by the United States government. "It is doubtful," one Indian writer declared in 1969, "that any nation will ever exceed the record of the

United States for perfidy."¹ The scene is studded with special villains, of whom President Andrew Jackson is perhaps the most infamous. A scholar of the early national period has written: "Jacksonian Indian policy was a blending of hypocrisy, cant, and rapaciousness, seemingly shot through with inconsistencies. Inconsistencies however are present only if the language of the presidential papers is taken seriously." In removing the Indians, this historian says, "the federal government had to display tact, cunning, guile, cajolery, and more than a hint of coercion. That it proved more than equal to the task was due in no small measure to Andrew Jackson's dedication to it. His performance was not that of responsible government official deferring to the will of constituents but rather that of a zealot who fully shared their biases and rapacity."²

We have been treated to a Marxist interpretation that claims, in the words of one writer, that "the *existence* of the United States is the result of the massive robbery of an entire continent and its resources from its aboriginal owners." According to this theory, "American Indians have experienced modern colonialism, that is, the expansion of the capitalist regimes into foreign areas, and capitalist exploitation of lands, resources and labor. American Indians have resisted colonialism using both defensive and offensive techniques. The United States as a socioeconomic and political entity is a result of that process. American Indian communities today are societies formed by their resistance to colonialism." Moreover, in this view, genocide was part and parcel of colonialism, and racism was "a principal ideological tool." The Marxists want us to consider Indian resistance

as class struggle and focus our attention on "the relationship of the indigenous peoples to capital, not just on the
cultural relationships of Europeans and Indians."[3]

On the other hand, practitioners of psychohistory
would have us believe that Indian policy can be explained
in Freudian or other psychoanalytical terms. "Replacing
Indians upon the land," one such historian has written,
"whites reunited themselves with nature. The rhetoric
of Manifest Destiny pictures America a 'young and growing country'; it expanded through 'swallowing territory,'
'just as an animal eats to grow.' Savagery would inevit-
ably 'be swallowed by' civilization. Whites imagina-
tively regressed, as they described expansion, to fantasies
of infant omnipotence," he says. "They entertained the
most primitive form of object relations, the annihilation
of the object through oral introjection." In this view,
whites infantilized Indians in order to regain parental
authority, which had been repressed in the liberal politics
of the day. Andrew Jackson's subjugation of the Indians,
in the same author's analysis, was a result of separation anxiety; Jackson proved his manhood by destroying
Indians.[4]

Of course these approaches to the history of the Indians
in the United States offer some truth, but they all exhibit
an *a priori* commitment to a set of principles, procrustean
beds on which to stretch the events and personalities of
the past. The first paints United States policy as black as
possible in order to make the Indians look as noble as
possible and thus hopes to win support for today's Indian
programs; it uses the past as a means to gain certain
ends in the present. The second is an ideological pattern
imposed upon the historical past, in which classes—
capitalists and workers—are set in opposition. The third

overemphasizes psychological categories in an attempt to delve deeply into the motivation of leaders (like Andrew Jackson) or whole societies (like the North as opposed to the South) in terms that might be understandable to Freudian aficionados today but that would have been incomprehensible to the people it tries to explain.

Now if the responsibility of historians is to understand the past, and understand it, too, in some measure, on its own terms, we must look at what the actors in the events said and did and examine the society in which they lived. We must be immersed as much as possible in the outlook of their times and grasp sympathetically the perceptions of the men and women who were responsible for directing the United States government in its relations with the American Indians. We cannot, therefore, write the history of Indian-white relations in the United States in terms of biological racism (as the twentieth century knows the concept), or in terms of extermination and physical genocide, or in terms of class struggle (colonialism or neocolonialism), or in terms of separation anxiety of national leaders and conflict between "anal" and "oral" societies.

Historians of Indian-white relations face the special problem of dealing with two diverse cultures, for we must understand two *others*, quite diverse in themselves. We realize that it is necessary to know something of the worldview of the Indians (because it is so different from our own), and we do not want to judge one culture by the norms of another. But we must also understand past white societies and not assume that the 1830s can be judged by the norms and values of the 1980s.

American society in the period from 1776 to 1920 was an heir of the Enlightenment. It believed in the power of human reason to fathom the principles of natural law and to organize society in accord with them. But it was even more a deeply religious society, in which a commitment to biblical truths and norms was assumed to be necessary for both individuals and the nation. Within these intellectual boundaries was fashioned an Indian policy that rested upon three fundamental principles.

The first was that all mankind was one, that all human beings were created innately equal by God and were descendants of one set of parents, Adam and Eve. Thus Thomas Jefferson believed in an essential, fixed human nature, unchangeable by time or place, and he wrote unequivocally in 1785: "I believe the Indian then to be in body and mind equal to the whiteman." If the circumstances of the Indians' environment could be changed, Jefferson thought, "we shall probably find that they are formed in mind as well as in body, on the same module with the 'Homo sapiens Europaeus.'"[5]

This view was the common one of the age, bolstered by a literal reading of Genesis. When, in the 1840s, the so-called American School of Ethnology proposed polygenesis—multiple creation of the races—and then argued that the separate creation of the nonwhite races accounted for innate inferiority of blacks and Indians, their innovations were rejected by the government officials who handled Indian affairs. Thomas L. McKenney, called by his modern biographer the "architect of America's early Indian policy," flatly rejected these first attempts at a scientific racism. He held firm to monogenesis and wrote in the 1840s:

> I am aware that opinions are entertained by some, embracing the theory of multiform creations; by such, the doctrine that

the whole family of man sprang from one original and common stock, is denied. There is, however, but one source whence information can be derived on this subject—and that is the Bible, and, until those who base their convictions on Bible testimony, consent to throw aside that great landmark of truth, they must continue in the belief that "the Lord God formed *man* of the dust of the ground, and breathed into his nostrils the breath of life, when he became a living soul." Being thus formed, and thus endowed, he was put by his creator in *the* garden, which was eastward, in Eden, whence flowed the river which parted, and became into four heads; and that from his fruitfulness his species were propagated.

The propagation of the entire human race from "an original pair," McKenney asserted, "is a truth so universally admitted, as to render any elaborate argument in its support superfluous." Since the Eden of Adam and Eve was not in America, the Indians could not have been indigenous to America. McKenney believed that the Indians were of Asiatic origin and had migrated to the New World by way of Bering Strait.[6]

The polygenesis of the American School, in fact, became a scientific oddity. The Indian reformers universally held to the identity of the Indian's human nature with that of the whites and thus to the reformability of the Indians. The commissioner of Indian affairs in 1868 asserted that "the fact stands out clear, well-defined, and indisputable, that Indians, not only as individuals but as tribes, are capable of civilization and of christianization." And one of his successors declared of Indian children in 1892: "They, too, are human and endowed with all the faculties of human nature; made in the image of God, being the likeness of their Creator, and having the same possibilities of growth and development that are possessed by any other class of children." He added, "The essential elements of human nature are the same in all [races] and in each, and the possibilities of development are limited only by the opportunities for growth and by culture forces."[7]

Even though unity of mankind with its corollary of innate equality of Indians and whites was firmly held and universally proclaimed by makers of Indian policy, a second principle must also be noted: The Indians in their existing cultural circumstances were inferior to the whites.

This inferiority was seen in many aspects of Indian life, for the whites (unaware of the concepts of cultural relativism and cultural pluralism that mark our own day) looked upon the Indians from a superior ethnocentric plateau. They saw cultures with primitive technologies, engaged in some limited agriculture yet dependent to a large extent upon hunting and gathering for food and apparel. It was common for white Americans to refer to Indian communities as hunter societies as opposed to white societies engaged in agriculture and domestic industries.[8] They saw pagan religion, and although they were no longer inclined (as had been the early Puritans) to see Satan immediately behind Indian beliefs and ceremonies, they compared the Indians' religions unfavorably with their own biblical Christianity. They contrasted the preliterate Indian societies (which had no written languages) with the accomplishments of their own society and judged the Indian languages generally worthless even though of scientific interest. They saw the increasing dependence of the Indians upon trade for the goods they had come to rely upon—guns and ammunition, kettles, knives, and other metal implements, and woven cloth— and they saw their own rapidly multiplying population overwhelming the static or declining numbers of the Indian tribes.

As early as 1803 Jefferson, who generally urged humanity in dealing with Indians but who was willing to fall back upon fear if need be, wrote to a territorial governor, "We presume that our strength and their weakness is now so visible, that they must see we have only to shut our hand to crush them." And as the years passed, the disparity between the Indian and white societies increased. Secretary of War John C. Calhoun in January 1820 noted "partial advances" made by the Indians, but he urged more radical measures and reported to Congress:

> They must be brought gradually under our authority and laws, or they will insensibly waste away in vice and misery. It is impossible, with their customs, that they should exist as independent communities, in the midst of civilized society. They are not, in fact, an independent people, (I speak of those surrounded by our population,) nor ought they to be so considered. They should be taken under our guardianship; and our opinion, and not theirs, ought to prevail, in measures intended for their civilization and happiness. A system less vigorous may protract, but cannot arrest their fate.[9]

According to the Jeffersonians, however, the Indians' inferiority was due to circumstances, not nature. The Jeffersonians and their intellectual heirs were committed environmentalists. The condition of the Indians, they were convinced, was due to their way of life. Commissioner of Indian Affairs T. Hartley Crawford noted in 1844 that the Indian race was "in no respect inferior to our own race, except in being less fortunately circumstanced." And Commissioner Thomas Jefferson Morgan insisted a half century later that "whatever of savagery or brutishness there has been in the history of [the Indian] people has been due rather to unfortunate circumstances, for which they were not always responsible, than to any inherent defect of nature. Under proper conditions the Indian baby grows into the cultivated, refined Christian gentleman or lovely woman."[10]

Hence the third fundamental principle: The Indians' culture could and should be transformed to equal or approximate that of their white neighbors. The inexorable progress exhibited in the history of human societies meant that the Indian would move through stages of society, from savagery to barbarism to ultimate civilization, just as the ancestors of the Europeans themselves had passed through those stages centuries ago. But Christian benevolence could not wait for the evolutionary progress to work itself out over centuries. It was the duty of Christians to speed up the process and to reform the Indian societies through positive and sometimes forcible means, the chief of which were instruction in agriculture and education in Christian schools.[11]

The outcome, as it took form in the Indian policy of the United States, can be expressed best by the word *paternalism*. Christian statesmen and their missionary allies looked upon the Indians as children toward whom they had a parental or paternal responsibility. It was the duty of parents to provide what was best for their minor children, look out for their best interests (which the children themselves could not judge), and assist the children to move to full maturity. A parallel concept was that of guardian and ward, in which the duties of the one toward the other rested upon what was almost a parent-child relationship. Guardian-ward was a legal relation, yet it had some of the connotations of love and religious concern that surrounded the common nineteenth-century view of parental or paternal responsibilities.

We need to note, of course, that paternalism could be either benevolent or oppressive. Parents tended to see it as benevolent; children often viewed the same actions as unduly restrictive. Since children were defenseless, they required assistance and support, and since children were not fully responsible, they required guidance. These ideas underlay the benevolent mode of paternalistic action, and they dominated the thought of humanitarian reformers who naively believed that with guidance and protection the Indians would move quickly toward their majority and take their place as independent citizens of the Republic. But this paternalism seemed never-ending, partly because, as the nation expanded westward, the United States government again and again came into contact with new groups of Indians, for whom the process was renewed; and partly because many Indians were slow to assume the mantle of full independence and self-sufficiency within the white man's world.

The more sinister connotations of paternalism are hinted at in the dictionary definition: "a policy or practice of treating or governing people in a fatherly manner, especially by providing for their needs without giving them responsibility." Worse still, children were ignorant; they could be deceived or treated in a way that served the interests of adults—a kind of exploitative paternalism.[12]

The paternalistic approach to Indian affairs was firmly in place by the time of Thomas Jefferson's administration. The object was to turn the Indian hunters into yeoman farmers (a policy that fitted well with Jefferson's agrarian propensities). If the Indians came to rely on agriculture and domestic manufacture for their food and clothing, they would no longer need extensive hunting grounds and would willingly give up their unneeded lands for white settlement (an outcome that fitted well with Jefferson's expansionism). Following the earlier example of George Washington and Henry Knox, Jefferson supported programs to promote agriculture and spinning and weaving among the tribes in close contact with white settlement, and he repeatedly urged his ideas upon the Indians who came east to meet with the Great Father. He told a group of Miami, Potawatomi, and Wea Indians in January 1802, "We shall with great pleasure see your people become disposed to cultivate the earth, to raise herds of useful animals and to spin and weave, for their food and clothing. These resources are certain, they will never disappoint you, while those of hunting may fail, and expose your women and children to the miseries of hunger and cold. We will with pleasure furnish you with implements for the most necessary arts, and with persons who may instruct [you] how to make and use them."[13]

Although it is possible to see Jefferson's motive simply as covetousness for Indian lands, such a view does violence to the thinking of the age. Jefferson and his contemporaries saw a mutual exchange between Indians and whites, as Jefferson himself told Congress: "In leading them thus to agriculture, to [domestic] manufacture, and civilization; in bringing together their and our sentiments, and preparing them ultimately to participate in the benefits of our Government, I trust and believe we are acting for their greatest good."[14]

The best exemplification of this Jeffersonian paternalistic bent in Indian policy was the work of Thomas

L. McKenney, a man of Quaker background who served
as superintendent of Indian trade from 1816 to 1822 and
then as the first head of the Indian Office, 1824–1830.
Although at first officially only superintendent of trade,
McKenney in fact made his office a center for humanitarian concern for the Indians, and he used his official
position to encourage the work of missionaries to the
Indians. He was especially interested in schools for Indian children, but he believed that all federal relations
with the tribes should be directed toward their civilization. He spoke of Indian affairs as "the great cause of
justice and benevolence"; his concern was to Christianize
and civilize the Indians as rapidly as possible, and he
regarded them as children who had to be guided on the
way. As head of the Indian Office he urged the Indians
to emigrate to western lands where they would be out of
contact with the vices of white society and could escape
the pressures on their lands. McKenney saw the program
he promoted as a triple one—emigration, preservation,
and improvement of the Indians—all suffused with a
paternal spirit.[15] Lamenting the sad condition of the Indians in their present situation, he wrote: "Seeing as I do
the condition of these people, and that they are bordering
on destruction, I would, were I empowered, take them
firmly but *kindly* by the hand, and tell them they must
go; and I would do this, on the same principle that I
would take my own children by the hand, firmly, but
kindly and lead them from a district of Country in which
the plague was raging."[16]

   McKenney was not alone in thinking of Indian emigration to the West in paternalistic terms. Whatever may
have been the purposes of the proponents of removal
(and some historians delight in charging them with all

sorts of evil motivation), the rhetoric of the age described the Indians as children or wards, in need of guidance from white officials who would work for their best interests. Even John Marshall in his landmark case of 1831, *Cherokee Nation* v. *Georgia,* spoke of the Indians as in "a state of pupilage" and declared that their relation to the United States "resembles that of a ward to his guardian." The Indians, he said, "look to our government for protection; rely upon its kindness and its power; appeal to it for relief to their wants; and address the president as their great father."[17]

Andrew Jackson, Marshall's great opponent on Indian removal as on other crucial issues, was especially forceful in justifying his position in terms of a father looking after his children. He wrote in 1829:

> You may rest assured that I shall adhere to the just and humane policy towards the Indians which I have commenced. In this spirit I have recommended them to quit their possessions on this side of the Mississippi, and go to a country to the west where there is every probability that they will always be free from the mercenary influence of White men, and undisturbed by the local authority of the states: Under such circumstances the General Government can exercise a parental control over their interests and possibly perpetuate their race.[18]

He saw removal of the Indians from the jurisdiction of the eastern states as a prelude to the government's "exercising such a general control over their affairs as may be essential to their interest and safety." In his Farewell Address of March 4, 1837, Jackson reverted to the same theme:

> This unhappy race—the original dwellers in our land—are now placed in a situation where we may well hope that they will

share in the blessings of civilization and be saved from that degradation and destruction to which they were rapidly hastening while they remained in the States; and while the safety and comfort of our own citizens have been greatly promoted by their removal, the philanthropist will rejoice that the remnant of that ill-fated race has been at length placed beyond the reach of injury or oppression, and that the paternal care of the General Government will hereafter watch over them and protect them.[19]

A superficial argument against the view of a paternalistic Indian policy was the use of treaties to deal with the Indian nations. The use of such formal instruments bespoke relations between equal sovereign political entities, not a parent-child relationship. While such a case might be made for the early years of the United States, when the emerging nation was faced by Indian tribes of considerable power, as the nineteenth century progressed, the treaty system changed radically in nature. Treaties (although retaining the old forms) became in fact instruments used by the United States government for its own purposes; treaties became instruments of American paternalism.

Why treaties continued to be used is easy enough to understand, for they were a convenient means ready at hand, and the treaty-making power of the federal government established by the Constitution was a principal support for centralized (rather than state) control of Indian affairs. To be sure, as early as 1817 Andrew Jackson, then commanding the Military Division of the South, questioned the wisdom of the traditional procedure and declared that to treat the Indians as though they were independent nations rather than simply subjects of the United States was nonsense. The treaty policy had grown up out of necessity, he argued, when the United States had been too weak to enforce its regulations among the Indians or keep peace in any other way. President Monroe and Secretary of War Calhoun approved Jackson's views, but Congress would not abandon the treaty system, which continued in force until 1871, modified in practice to serve the purposes of the federal government.[20]

Treaties became civilizing instruments intended by the federal government to move the Indians from their aboriginal cultural patterns to the agricultural existence that was deemed necessary for the Indians. Elements of Indian policy were embedded in the treaties, which were then presented to the Indians in council for their acquiescence. It is tempting to view this simply as a fraud, to characterize the treaties, as Commissioner of Indian Affairs Francis A. Walker did in the early 1870s, as "a mere form to amuse and quiet savages, a half-compassionate, half-contemptuous humoring of unruly children."[21] But that would be to ignore the strong strains of benevolent paternalism that shine through the numerous treaties made with the Indians in mid-century.

We can take as one example the series of treaties signed in the 1850s, as the United States sought to open up new areas in the Trans-Mississippi West to white settlement and exploitation. Regardless of the tribes concerned—whether Plains Indians in Kansas, salmon fishermen in the Pacific Northwest, or the Utes of New Mexico—the treaties contained set provisions aimed at transforming cultural patterns in order to enable the Indians to survive and prosper under the new circumstances of American expansion. These were (1) reduction of the Indian landholdings and designation of limited reservations, either as part of the old lands or in entirely new locations; (2) provision of farm-sized plots of land for individual Indian families, to be allotted by the president in severalty; (3) annuities that (at the discretion of the president) could be expended for education and other means to civilization; and (4) grants for establishing farms and building mills and blacksmith shops, and employment for a set period of years of millers, blacksmiths, and farmers.[22] That these treaties were imposed upon the Indians increased rather than lessened the paternalistic impact. "The Great Father felt for his children—he pitied them," Governor Isaac I. Stevens told the Indians in Washington Territory, "and he has sent me here to-day to express those feelings, and to make a Treaty for your benefit." Stevens's wife wrote that the Indians "think so much of the whites that a child can govern them." Her husband, she said, had them "right under his thumb—they are afraid as death of him and do just as he tells them."[23]

Another set of treaties was negotiated with the Indians by the United States Indian Peace Commission in 1867 and 1868. The commission was authorized by Congress in 1867 to take whatever steps were necessary to end the warfare on the plains by responding to the grievances the Indians had. The group comprised civilian officials and high-ranking military men; it was chaired by the commissioner of Indian affairs, Nathaniel G. Taylor, who epitomized the paternalistic outlook of Washington officialdom. Taylor was a Methodist minister as well as a politician, and he sought the "civilization" of the Indians with a vengeance. A newspaper correspondent aptly said of him: "He writes poetry, has a fine command of chaste English, wears a wig, preaches occasionally at Washington, D.C., and is a most gentlemanly man, possessed of many scholarly traits. In reference to the Indian question he is inclined to be the red man's friend; in fact, few men with so warm a heart as his could very well be otherwise."[24]

As the Peace Commission went about its work, holding councils with Indians in southern Kansas and along the upper Missouri, the talks its members repeated to the assembled tribal leaders made clear beyond any shadow of doubt the purposes the Peace Commission had in mind. Thus Taylor told the Crow Indians at Fort Laramie that the government desired to set reservations apart for them:

> Upon the reservations you select, we propose to build a house for your agent to live in, to build a mill to saw your timber, and a mill to grind your wheat and corn, when you raise any; a blacksmith shop and a house for your farmer, and such other buildings as may be necessary. We also propose to furnish to you homes and cattle, to enable you to begin to raise a supply of stock with which to support your families when the game has disappeared. We desire also to supply you with clothing to make you comfortable and all necessary farming implements so that you can make your living by farming. We will send you teachers for your children.[25]

The Indians did not agree with this dream of a rosy agricultural future, for they wanted to continue their free life of buffalo hunting, but their views made little imprint on the minds of the commissioners. Another member of the commission, John B. Sanborn, told the Oglala Sioux: "The President desires to see you prosperous and happy and has sent us here to devise means to secure this end. We have exercised our best judgment and adopted the best plan to improve your condition and save your people. Accept it and be happy."[26]

The treaties negotiated by the Indian Peace Commission represented this "best judgment" and were at the heart civilizing treaties. So much has been made of the reservation and land-cession provisions of the treaties (notably the Fort Laramie Treaty of 1868) that the plan for the Indians on the reservations has been all but forgotten. These treaties were reformist documents, aimed at attaining the humanitarian goals of the commission and the government, although the reforming tendencies were no doubt little understood by the Indians.[27]

The treaty system ended in 1871, when Congress decided that no more treaties would be made with Indian tribes (although old treaties would stay in force), but the paternalism of the federal government toward the Indians continued. In fact, it acquired new life with the inauguration of the post–Civil War reforms known as Grant's peace policy.

The first step in that new policy was the creation of a lay board to advise the Indian Office and serve as a watchdog that might lessen or eliminate the fraud and corruption for which the Indian Office had become notorious. The ten members appointed to this Board of Indian Commissioners by Grant were a remarkable collection of high-minded Christian philanthropists, suffused with a spirit of benevolence, who epitomized the evangelical religious atmosphere of the nineteenth century. For better or for worse, the American Indians fell into the hands of this group and their successors.[28]

The board, in its first annual report in 1869, even before it had had time to get much firsthand experience with Indian affairs, drew up a blueprint that comprised all the elements of federal Indian policy for the next half century. The report reflected the common wisdom of the age regarding what to do about the Indian problem and was to a great extent an *a priori* approach, coming from the benevolence of a kindly group of religiously committed men who were convinced that they knew what was best for the Indians. The proposals became staple elements in federal relations with the Indians and persisted through the Indian wars that, paradoxically, coincided with the peace policy.[29]

The board urged that the Indians be collected on small contiguous reservations, with the idea that the whole would become one large unit and eventually enter the Union as a state. The reservation lands should be given to the Indians in severalty and tribal relations discouraged. Money annuities should cease, for they promoted idleness and vice. The board urged the establishment of schools to teach the children English and wanted teachers nominated by religious bodies. Christian missions, too, should be encouraged and their schools fostered. "The religion of our blessed Savior," the members said, "is believed to be the most effective agent for the civilization of any people." Agents and other employees of the Indian service were to be appointed "with a view to their moral as well as business qualifications, and aside from any political consideration."

Although the board insisted on an honest observance of treaty obligations, it wanted ultimately to abandon the treaty system and to abrogate existing treaties as soon as a just method could be devised. "The legal status of the uncivilized Indians," it decided, "should be that of wards of the government; the duty of the latter being to protect them, to educate them in industry, the arts of civilization, and the principles of Christianity; elevate them to the rights of citizenship, and to sustain and clothe them until they can support themselves."

To accomplish this benevolent program, the Indian reservations from 1870 to 1882 were taken out of the hands of political appointees and army officers and actually placed under the control of Christian church bodies, which nominated the agents and other field employees and sought by the goodness of the personnel to reform the Indian service and transform the Indians.[30]

These idealistic elements of the peace policy did not prosper in the Gilded Age. Conflicts between the Board of Indian Commissioners and the Department of the Interior over the board's authority weakened the direct influence of the board in Indian affairs, and the church-appointed agents proved unsatisfactory, to a large extent because of bickering between the religious denominations about who should control which agencies. But the thrust of the peace policy was not diverted from its primary goals of rapid civilization and Christianization of the Indians. Even the military men, who sought unsuccessfully in the late 1860s and 1870s to wrest control of Indian affairs away from the civilian officials of the Interior Department, differed little from their opponents in the ultimate programs they proposed for the Indians.

As the structures of the peace policy weakened and collapsed, the dominating influence on Indian affairs came from Carl Schurz, who served as secretary of the interior under President Hayes from 1877 to 1881. Schurz was a hardheaded realist as well as a reformer, and his firm convictions about dealing with Indians were as paternalistic as those of the Christian philanthropists. In summing up the state of Indian affairs at the end of his tenure, Schurz aptly encapsulated the official thought of his day.

He believed in the ability of the Indians to move down the path to white civilization and citizenship, but he insisted that they must be carefully directed to the goal. "Nothing is more indispensable than the protecting and guiding care of the Government during the dangerous period of transition from savage to civilized life," he wrote. Schurz saw the wild hunter turning to the new ways. "He feels himself like a child in need of leading-strings," he said. " . . . He is overcome by a feeling of helplessness, and he naturally looks to the 'Great Father' to take him by the hand and guide him on. That guiding hand must necessarily be one of authority and power to command confidence and respect. It can be only that of the government which the Indian is accustomed to regard as a sort of omnipotence on the earth. Everything," Schurz added, "depends upon the wisdom and justice of that guidance." And he spoke of the government exercising "paternal functions [toward the Indians] until they are sufficiently advanced to take care of themselves."[31]

Schurz's statement coincided with the beginning of the massive agitation for Indian reform that dominated the last two decades of the nineteenth century. When the Indian wars ended, the subjugated Indians, crushed in spirit and impounded on reservations, fell into the hands of a zealous group of men and women who were the culmination of the humanitarian movement that had developed through the century. Organized into voluntary associations like the Women's National Indian Association and the Indian Rights Association and meeting annually as the Lake Mohonk Conference of Friends of the Indian, these Christian men and women were absolutely sure that they knew what was best for the Indians. They brought into a new focus the scattered threads of reform, and they exhibited a paternalism run rampant.[32]

These groups insisted first of all that the Indians throw over their traditional tribalism with its communal emphasis and adopt the individualism that marked white society. To accomplish this the reformers had a three-part formula: (1) the reservations (which they correctly perceived to be the basis of tribal community life) must be broken up and the land allotted in severality to individual Indians in parcels of 80, 160, or 320 acres; (2) the individual Indians must be made subject to white laws and ultimately accept the rights and duties of American citizenship; and (3) the Indian children must be educated in English-speaking schools, not only in the three R's but in vocational skills and in patriotic citizenship.

Unable to resist this cultural onslaught, the Indians to a large extent succumbed. Under the provisions of the Dawes Act of 1887, many reservations were broken up into allotments and the surplus lands were sold to the government for white settlement. As owners of private property, to be developed and bequeathed to heirs, the Indians were supposed to adopt the Puritan work ethic, demand legal protection of their rights, and support education for their children. When Indians received their allotments under the act, they became citizens of the United States. In the 1890s a national government school system for the Indians was inaugurated—the inspiration of Thomas Jefferson Morgan, commissioner of Indian affairs under President Benjamin Harrison and the darling of the Lake Mohonk Conference. "The whole tendency of modern legislation in providing for the allotment of lands in severalty and the conferring of citizenship upon

Indians," Morgan wrote, "has been toward greater freedom for the Indians and a more careful respect for their
individual rights. Nothing but the sternest necessity can
warrant the Government in deviating from this more
humane policy until it shall have accomplished its benign
work of the complete enfranchisement of these people."[33]

The purpose of the legislation of the late-nineteenth-
century reformers—land in severalty, citizenship, and
education—was to make the Indians self-supporting and
assimilate them into the general population. Then there
would be no more "Indian problem," for there would be
no more persons identified as Indians. The Indian Office
would wither away, and government paternalism toward
the Indians would be at an end. Some reformers san-
guinely predicted that this would be a matter of only one
generation.

What actually happened, instead, was a multiplication
of employees in the Indian service and a proportionate
increase in the government's direction of the Indians'
lives. This came about, primarily, because of the individualization of the Indians, which led not to rapid self-
sufficiency but to continuing and in some cases almost
total dependence upon the federal government. Instead
of dealing with tribal entities, which in turn were responsible for members of the tribe, the Indian Office, having
weakened or destroyed the tribal organization, now had
to deal directly with tens of thousands of individual and
dependent Indians—with the allottees, the students, and
individual Indians who needed medical care.

The result was total wardship for the Indians, which
was recognized and lamented by officials in the government, but which no one seemed able to lessen. Commis-

sioner of Indian Affairs William Jones saw this clearly in 1901. "Certainly it is time to make a move toward terminating the guardianship which has so long been exercised over the Indians and putting them upon an equal footing with the white man so far as their relations with the Government are concerned," he wrote in his annual report. "Under the present system the Indian ward never attains his majority. The guardianship goes on in an unbroken line from father to son, and generation after generation the Indian lives and dies a ward."[34] Jones had an obsession about self-support for the Indians, and he condemned past policies and practices that he believed prevented the Indians from attaining their majority, but the general situation changed little or not at all as the result of his efforts.

More than a dozen years later Commissioner Cato Sells had a similar complaint and noted the deleterious results of the system. He wrote:

> The Government's policy has been to coddle the restricted Indian [that is, the one whose land was held in trust], transact his business for him, do his thinking for him, giving him no opportunity to grow strong by assuming responsibility, and then suddenly, after he has become thoroughly emasculated from nonuse of his powers, when he has obtained a certain knowledge of the English language in the schools, restrictions have been removed from his property, and in most cases it has been quickly dissipated.[35]

Yet Sells was paternalistic at heart, despite his extensive policy of removing from federal guardianship those Indians who were found to be "competent." He wanted to involve the Indians in planning social services for them because the planners required "a clear comprehension of the viewpoint of those served." But he quickly took away with his left hand what he offered with his right. "Oftentimes," he noted, "the Indian's objection to various plans made on his behalf may be based on minor considerations which can be eliminated easily to the satisfaction of the Indian and without seriously interfering with the successful outcome of *the plans devised for his interests*."[36]

It is true that in the early decades of the twentieth century many Indians were rapidly—indeed almost recklessly—pushed into independence. Those who were considered able to stand on their own feet received full control of their property and were removed from the lists of Indians for whom the government offered protection and guidance. But it was also clear that thousands of Indians were not yet competent to handle their own affairs. For these the federal government continued its guardianship, and its supervision became more and more detailed, as provisions for health, schools, and management of Indian land and funds multiplied. Sells's superior, Secretary of the Interior John Barton Payne, grasped the situation well. "It may take the Indians a very long, long time to become really competent," he told Sells at the end of 1920; "but we should be patient and not permit ourselves to be hurried. . . . [F]or a long time yet the Indians must continue the wards of the nation, and the nation must take care of them."[37]

Thus as the Indians lost their traditional way of life, they became increasingly dependent upon the Great Father for subsistence, for education, and for health care. As their tribal organization was weakened and the influence of the traditional elders and chiefs denigrated, decision-making about their lives was more and more assumed by the Indian agents and other government officials. According to the accepted wisdom of the day, the Indians would remain in need of help until they were all, at length, completely assimilated.

2
Dependency

Paternalism toward the Indians was not projected out of some conscious or unconscious needs of the whites, nor was it developed simply as a rationalization for crass materialistic gain. It grew out of a genuine, though often misguided, desire to aid peoples seen as inferior and dependent—to bring to them the "blessings of Christian civilization."

We know that historical circumstances and events are complex, the result of the interplay of many forces, and that simple answers tend to be distorted answers. We know, too, that not all Indian groups were the same and that great variations obtained in regard to political and economic power. Yet it seems clear that paternalism flourished through the decades because the Indians were in fact dependent and that they became more and more dependent as the nineteenth century unfolded, that their state of dependency called forth paternalistic responses on the part of the federal government, and that the paternalism in turn caused still further dependence.

Let us see how that was so, looking at restrictions upon Indian political independence, at the loss of Indian economic self-sufficiency and the resultant dependence upon the whites for existence, and at the total wardship status of the Indians under the reservation system.

The condition of the Indians changed through the decades, and dependency hit different tribes at different times. But by the end of the nineteenth century the autonomy and self-sufficiency of all the Indian tribes had been radically diminished. Declining from a position of prosperity and of considerable political and economic power at the beginning of the national history of the United States, the Indian tribes by the early decades of the twentieth century had become politically subordinate to and almost completely dominated by the federal government; they were economically dependent, too, upon white goods and services.

If we go back to the end of the European colonial period, we can see that the major Indian nations on the frontiers of white settlement then played an important diplomatic role. The anthropologist Edward H. Spicer, in his illuminating book *A Short History of the Indians of the United States,* speaks of the "many nations" in the seventeenth and eighteenth centuries—Indian nations and European nations (in their colonial extensions)—vying for trade advantages, for land, and for political power. A great majority of the Indians were not yet subordinated politically or dominated culturally. Most of them, except for the weakened and disintegrating eastern tribes, operated in a political arena where they could maintain their accustomed independence through fighting or negotiation and even win additional power over other Indians. One needs only to think of the Six Nations of the Iroquois Confederacy (the Mohawks and Senecas, for example) or the powerful and diplomatically astute southern nations (such as the Creeks and the Cherokees) to confirm the point. At the beginning of the eighteenth century the Europeans recognized fifty or sixty Indian "nations," whom both they and the Indians considered distinct political groups. At the same time there were a variety of European "nations"—French, Dutch, Spanish, and British (often broken down into distinct colonies, which multiplied the political entities with whom the Indian nations had to deal).[1]

After the Revolutionary War, with a considerable sense of urgency, the United States signed treaties of peace with the Iroquois at Fort Stanwix, New York, with the southern tribes at Hopewell, South Carolina, and with the Indians north of the Ohio at Fort McIntosh. The use of treaties, carried over from British practice, was a compelling indication that the Indians were considered to be nations.

Yet the Indians' situation had already changed substantially, no matter what diplomatic forms still persisted. The many nations operating in terms of rough equality were being replaced by a single dominant nation, the United States. The French, defeated by the British in the Seven Years' War, by the Peace of Paris in 1763 had withdrawn from North America. The Spanish at the same time had moved west beyond the Mississippi River (although they regained Florida in 1783); and with the patriots' victory over the British in the Revolutionary War, the United States became the master of the territory stretching from the Great Lakes to Florida and from the Atlantic Ocean to the Mississippi River. It is true that Indian tribes could still look for succor from sympathetic British agents in the north and from Spanish officials in the south, but Jay's Treaty with England in 1794 and the Treaty of San Lorenzo with Spain in 1795 weakened the influence of these two European imperial powers, and the trans-Mississippi region became American with the Louisiana Purchase in 1803.

In the War of 1812, the Indians were defeated in both the north and the south, despite their hopes for aid from Great Britain, and the Treaty of Ghent signaled the end of any further hope of holding back the new behemoth. The Indians east of the Mississippi were well aware that they were in a desperate struggle to escape domination and that their way of life as well as their lands was threatened. The failure of the great Shawnee chief Tecumseh to establish a confederacy of Indian tribes supported by the British, to resist American advance, in a way had sealed their doom, for Tecumseh was trying to reverse a movement that had already gathered significant momentum.

The initial treaties with the Indians after the Revolution had themselves made clear the acceptance by the Indians of the paramount political role of the United States. Thus the Treaty of Hopewell with the Cherokees (November 28, 1785) asserted: "The said Indians for themselves and their respective tribes and towns do acknowledge all the Cherokees to be under the protection of the United States of America, and of no other sovereign whosoever." And the Indians agreed that "for the benefit and comfort of the Indians, and for the prevention of injuries or oppressions on the part of the citizens or Indians, the United States in Congress assembled shall have the sole and exclusive right of regulating the trade with the Indians, and managing all their affairs in such manner as they think proper." Other treaties of the time and subsequent treaties, too, made similar assertions without significant or effective Indian remonstrance.[2] The Indian trade and intercourse laws, moreover, established the dominance of the United States in the external affairs of the tribes.[3]

It was this situation that Chief Justice John Marshall

eloquently described in the case of *Cherokee Nation* v. *Georgia* in 1831:

> The Indian territory is admitted to compose a part of the United States. In all our maps, geographical treatises, histories, and laws, it is so considered. In all our intercourse with foreign nations, in our commercial regulations, in any attempt at intercourse between Indians and foreign nations, they are considered as within the jurisdictional limits of the United States, subject to many of those restraints which are imposed upon our own citizens. . . . They and their country are considered by foreign nations, as well as by ourselves, as being so completely under the sovereignty and dominion of the United States, that any attempt to acquire their lands, or to form a political connexion with them, would be considered by all as an invasion of our territory, and an act of hostility.[4]

The political dominance of the United States that resulted from victories over Great Britain in 1783 and 1815 as well as from concomitant defeats of Indians during the War of 1812 was matched by the growing power that came from population growth. In 1790, the year of the first federal census, the United States counted 3,929,000 persons. In 1810 the census showed 7,224,000; and by 1830, 12,901,000. Twenty years later, at mid-century, the population of the United States stood at 23,261,000, the thirteen original states had increased to thirty-one, the frontier line of white settlement had jumped across the Mississippi to the ninety-eighth meridian, and there were sizable population centers in Texas and on the Pacific coast. While this phenomenal white growth occurred, the Indian nations declined. The Indian population in 1850 was perhaps 350,000.[5]

A dramatic and often decisive role in this population decline was played by devastating epidemics of European diseases. Isolated for millennia in the New World, the

Indians had developed no immunity to common Old World diseases that were seldom fatal to the whites—measles, scarlet fever, and whooping cough, for example. More serious diseases like smallpox and cholera, which hit white settlements, too, in some cases almost wiped out Indian communities. The epidemics, carrying off large segments of population, weakened the Indian economic systems and dispirited the people, whose world order seemed to have collapsed in the face of unknown forces.[6]

Population size, of course, was not the only—or even the most important—factor, for small nations could and did survive among the nations of the world. Many Indians and their white friends maintained that the proper status of the Indian tribes was as small independent nations under the protection of the United States. John Marshall made use of this argument in *Worcester* v. *Georgia* when he asserted: "The settled doctrine of the law of nations is, that a weaker power does not surrender its independence—its right to self-government, by associating with a stronger, and taking its protection. A weak state, in order to provide for its safety, may place itself under the protection of one more powerful, without stripping itself of the right of government, and ceasing to be a state."[7] One could argue, too, that the Five Civilized Tribes in the Indian Territory (present-day Oklahoma) had in fact achieved that status.

But such a protectorate system requires that the weaker state have substantial internal autonomy and self-sufficiency. For most of the Indian tribes, that condition disappeared because with the coming of the Europeans they could no longer maintain their age-old subsistence patterns intact. The tribes, once self-sufficient, were transformed into groups dependent upon the market economy of the whites. This radical revolution has only recently received careful attention from historians, who are learning to work in ecological and environmental history as well as in the more traditional forms of political and economic history.[8]

The aboriginal societies that the Indians had developed in relation to their environments—whether hunting and gathering societies or semiagricultural communities—worked on a reciprocal and self-sustaining basis. Land and other resources were gifts of nature to be used, not commodities to be accumulated for profit and power. Political leaders were those who successfully managed an equitable distribution of the fruits of the earth. We must not, in a romantic mood, picture these communities as idyllic, for bad seasons and warfare brought hardship and misery, but the mixed hunting-gathering-horticultural system of the Indians was a stable one. The goal of production was economic security, not maximized use of resources, and security was achieved by diversity of production.[9]

White contact changed these Indian economies and in some cases destroyed them. We can see this by a brief glance at three examples.

In New England, when the first white men came to settle, they encountered Indian communities that had established workable relationships with the environment. Those in southern New England, where the English concentrated their settlements, had a partly agricultural, partly hunting-gathering economy, which provided subsistence for the population. Moving through cycles of plenty and want, the Indians exploited the seasonal diversity of the region by seasonal mobility, as they balanced their cultivated crops with hunting and gathering of wild foodstuffs. These patterns were largely destroyed by the invading English, who established permanent settlements, bounded the land with fences and private ownership, and transformed the ecosystems on which the Indians had built their subsistence economies. The Indians were drawn into the market network of the English and became increasingly dependent upon the white society as their traditional means of survival disappeared. The fur trade, for example, revolutionized the Indian economy by a new commercialism, which soon threatened the supply of animals. And the expanding and fenced lands of the English settlers eroded the land base on which the Indians had depended.[10]

Similarly, the Choctaw Indians in the southeastern United States, before white contact, had developed a mixture of agriculture and hunting, the combination of which provided reasonable security if not abundance. The chief's primary obligation was generosity in the distribution of goods acquired in communal hunting and agriculture, and this reciprocal system was a mainstay of Choctaw life.

The coming of the whites not only changed the ecological basis on which the Choctaws had lived, but European trade goods became necessities for the Indians, and the market system ensnared them. They now hunted deer, not for a secure subsistence to augment their agriculture, but for skins to trade to the English or French for guns or liquor. The chiefs desperately needed European goods to distribute to their tribesmen if they were to maintain their positions of authority and prestige. It was a gradual process, but in the end the Choctaws succumbed. Their traditional economy collapsed in the face of the new market economy, and older leaders gave place to mixed-bloods who understood the new system and operated within it. A recent study of the transition among the Choctaws concludes: "The market and liquor emptied the forests of game; they brought into the nation the white traders who intermarried, pushed cattle herds into the borderlands, and started cotton plantations. . . . For the Choctaws as a whole, trade and market meant not wealth but impoverishment, not well-being but dependency, and not progress but exile and dispossession. They never fought the Americans; they were never conquered. Instead, through the market they were made dependent and dispossessed."[11]

A third and compelling example of the decline to dependency is that of the Teton Sioux in Dakota. In 1850 they had been masters of the northern plains and had dominated the treaty conference at Fort Laramie in 1851. Only thirty years later, in 1880, they were living on reservations, settled there against their will. Warfare, which had been a dominant activity and one by which men achieved prestige, wealth, and rank, was gone. The tribal economy based on the buffalo hunts also disappeared. The vanishing herds—destroyed by white hunters for their hides—symbolized the vanishing way of life; and traditional diet, clothing, lodging, and other cultural objects were no more. Rations and annuity goods replaced the buffalo as the principal source of material goods.[12] Politically, too, many of the old forms were shattered, and the government Indian agent became increasingly dominant against the chiefs and warriors on the reservation. To top it all, the government organized a crusade against Indian religious and social customs.

The result for the Sioux was poverty, despondency, and almost despair—and a dependency that was nearly absolute.

Still another factor was involved in the movement toward dependency: the technological revolution that the European invasion brought to Indian lives. The Indians of America north of Mexico, when Columbus stumbled upon the New World, were fundamentally Stone Age peoples. They had no domesticated animals except the dog and no metal tools; most had no woven garments. Then came the whites with a technological mastery that the Indians lacked, with horses and cattle and sheep, with steel knives and copper kettles, with cotton cloth and woolen blankets—and with guns and gunpowder. Some of these elements of European culture were adopted by the Indians and worked into their own subsistence patterns. The dramatic instance, of course, was the horse; animals and techniques were taken over by the Indians of the Southwest from the Spanish and then rapidly diffused north and northeast until by the middle of the eighteenth century the Plains Indians had been transformed into nomadic horsemen. Similarly, the sheep first acquired from the Spanish became a mainstay of the Navajo Indians, and use of wool for spinning and weaving of rugs and blankets became a mark of those Indians.

But many Indians, adopting the knives, axes, hoes, kettles, and blankets, to say nothing of beads, mirrors, and other ornaments, became dependent upon the whites for these trade goods. Of signal importance was the gun, as a hunting tool to replace spears and bows and arrows and as a military weapon (a new force in continuing tribal warfare). As these manufactured goods changed from

luxuries or novelties to absolute necessities, the Indians
became caught .in the white man's economic network.
Granted this dependence upon tools and other items,
there were two alternatives: The Indians themselves could
learn to produce the artifacts, or they must obtain them
from the whites. As to domestic animals—horses and
sheep—the Indians became self-sufficient, breeding and
adapting the animals for their own uses. As to manufactured goods, the Indians never learned to produce, or
even to repair, their own. Here was an economic dependency of far-reaching scope, which increased as environmental changes made the European goods increasingly
important. (For example, as hunting grounds were depleted, guns—more effective than bows and arrows—
became indispensable for providing subsistence from
hunting.)

As early as 1772, Choctaw chiefs in council with the
English abjectly acknowledged their helplessness as they
pleaded for English goods. "We are poor and Incapable
of making Necessaries for ourselves," said one great
medal chief, and another asserted that the Choctaws were
"Ignorant and helpless as the Beasts in the woods[.]
Incapable of making Necessaries for ourselves[,] our sole
dependence is upon you."[13]

The dependence of the Indians on trade or on presents
was early recognized by officials of the United States.
Lewis Cass, governor of Michigan Territory, in 1816
spoke of a moral obligation to provide for the Indians
who had given up "the fairest portion of their Country"
to the whites and who now found it difficult to subsist
by hunting alone. Without the annual presents they had
come to expect from the government, Cass found it
"difficult to conceive how they could support and clothe

themselves." When Cass and William Clark, superintendent of Indian affairs at St. Louis, were called upon by the secretary of war in 1829 to draw up regulations for the Indian department, they noted unequivocally: "The time when the Indians generally could supply themselves with food and clothing, without any of the articles of civilized life, has long since passed away."[14]

The French observer Alexis de Tocqueville remarked sharply on this Indian dependency in the early 1830s:

> When the Indians alone dwelt in the wilderness from which now they are driven, their needs were few. They made their weapons themselves, the water of the rivers was their only drink, and the animals they hunted provided them with food and clothes.
>
> The Europeans introduced firearms, iron, and brandy among the indigenous population of North America; they taught it to substitute our cloth for the barbaric clothes which had previously satisfied Indian simplicity. While contracting new tastes, the Indians did not learn the arts to gratify them, and they had to have recourse to the industry of the whites. In return for these goods, which they did not know how to make, the savages could offer nothing but the rich furs still abounding in their forests. From that time forward hunting had to provide not only for their own needs but also for the frivolous passions of Europe. They no longer hunted for forest animals simply for food, but in order to obtain the only things they could barter with us.[15]

The Indians' need for trade goods was used by the white governments from early times for political ends. It had been clearly recognized by the European colonial governments that trade was the great means of cementing political alliances—that the Indians would support in war those upon whom they depended for trade—and the United States played the same game. In early years government officials worried about how to divert the Indian trade from British to American traders and how to provide adequately for the Indians' wants. The government trading houses established in President Washington's administration and eagerly fostered by Jefferson and others were intended, as Washington said, "to conciliate their [the Indians'] attachment." The federal government hoped by its trading-house system to drive out the private traders. If that were done, the United States would have power to control the actions of the Indians by granting or withholding supplies. All these political maneuverings were based on the fact that the Indians had become fundamentally dependent upon white goods.[16]

The Plains Indians, too, suffered technological dependency. As long as the buffalo still existed, the Indians continued to hunt them. For that activity guns and ammunition had become essential, but the whites controlled the supply of firearms. When the United States Indian Peace Commission treated with the Plains Indians in 1867 and 1868, its goal was to persuade the Indians to give up their old ways and settle down on reservations in an agricultural life, to become civilized in the white man's pattern of subsistence. The Indians wanted none of it. While the commissioners were extolling the benefits of a peaceful life as farmers, the Indians looked for a continuing supply of guns and powder so that they could still profit from the hunt. The whites wanted to withhold the weapons, in large part because they feared that the guns would be used in warfare against the whites, but also because they hoped by destroying reliance on the buffalo to induce or force the Indians to farm.

In pitiable scenes the Indians pleaded with the commissioners. Black Foot of the Crows said at Fort Laramie in 1867: "You speak of putting us on a reservation and teaching us to farm. We were not brought up to that and are not able to do it. The talk does not please us. We want horses to run after the game and guns and ammunition to kill it. I would like to live just as I have been raised." The Sioux chief Spotted Tail echoed those sentiments. "Now we want to live as our fathers have lived, on the buffalo and the deer that we now find on our hunting grounds," he said. "We love to roam over the plains. We love our wigwams. We love to hunt. We do not want to live like the white man. The Indian cannot be a white man. We are men like you, but the Great Spirit gave us hunting grounds, gave us the buffalo, the elk, the deer, and the antelope. Our fathers have taught us to hunt and live on the Plains and we are contented."[17]

But the old life now required guns and lead and powder. Man That Walks under Ground, an Oglala Sioux, admitted their dependency. "I am an Indian and cannot make powder," he said. "We cannot make balls and caps, and in what direction shall we go to make peace and to live happy, unless we can get ammunition from you?"[18]

Indian dependency increased as the traditional means of survival were weakened and destroyed in the passage of time. When land cessions depleted hunting grounds and the bounty of fur-bearing animals disappeared, annuities received by the Indians in payment for land replaced the fur trade in supplying what the Indians required. It was a more insidious form of dependence, for annuities, whether in goods or in money, required no work on the part of the Indians, who came to live on the annuities and on the supplementary rations often supplied by the government as a kind of dole.

For the Plains Indians the loss of economic independence came later than it did for the eastern tribes, but it was just as inexorable. Greatly weakened by loss of their buffalo supplies, they at length succumbed to the military power of the United States and were forced to reservations just as their brothers in the East and in the Far West had been. Custer's defeat in 1876 was but a brief moment of glory for the Sioux and the Cheyennes, and Chief Joseph's Nez Perces provided new excitement in their attempt to flee pursuing white soldiers in 1877. But Joseph's reputed surrender speech could serve for all the Indians: "Hear me, my chiefs, I am tired; my heart is sick and sad. From where the sun now stands I will fight no more forever."[19]

By the time the Indians were crushed militarily, they had already lost their status as independent political entities, which could deal with the United States through treaties. For a long time there had been grumbling on the part of whites that the treaty system had become an absurdity. Even early in the nineteenth century perceptive men had seen the incongruity of treating the Indian tribes as equals; and after the Civil War the grumblings became a full chorus. The staunch Indian advocate Bishop Henry B. Whipple lamented in 1864 that "we treat as an independent nation a people whom we will not permit to exercise one single element of that sovereign power which is necessary to a nation's existence." And Ely S. Parker, the Seneca Indian who served as President Grant's commissioner of Indian affairs, insisted in 1869 that the treaty system be scrapped, since it falsely impressed upon the tribes a notion of national independence. "It is time," Parker said, "that this idea should be dispelled, and the government cease the cruel farce of thus dealing with its helpless and ignorant wards."[20]

The end came in 1871, occasioned by a squabble between the two houses of Congress, as the House of Representatives complained that it was denied a part in managing Indian affairs because it had no part in the treaty-making process. In an obscure section of the Indian appropriation bill, Congress declared that "hereafter no Indian nation or tribe within the territory of the United States shall be acknowledged or recognized as an independent nation, tribe, or power with whom the United States may contract by treaty," although it acknowledged the continuing validity of existing treaties.[21]

The internal affairs of the Indian tribes, it is true, were not directly affected by the legislation, but here too the tribes were unable to resist federal encroachment on their autonomy. Most notably, by the Major Crimes Act of 1885, Congress made certain serious criminal acts committed by Indians federal crimes and took them out of the jurisdiction of the tribes themselves.[22]

As the nineteenth century neared its close, the Indians on the reservations became almost completely dependent, a dependency that paradoxically was intensified by the very programs and policies that the paternalistic government of the United States instituted to assist the dependent Indians.

The reservations at first were considered to be "hothouses," in which the civilization programs of the Indian Office could prosper under ideal conditions. There the

Indians would be gathered into concentrated population masses, where schools and churches could flourish
and where the agricultural skills that were needed for
the transformation of the Indians into yeoman farmers
could be taught. It was a tightly controlled environment in which the politically appointed Indian agent was
supreme.

Schoolmasters—often supplied by missionary societies
—inculcated patriotic American citizenship; agency physicians sought to cure disease and simultaneously deni-
grate the traditional medicine men; agency farmers,
blacksmiths, and other artisans promoted cultivation of
crops; and agency police, at the command of the agent,
preserved law and order. Under such regulated conditions, the environmentalist officials and reformers hoped
to produce a new generation of Indians who, having
thrown over their old ways and the tribal authorities that
supported them, could fend for themselves in the white
man's world as self-supporting individuals and families.

The programs were duly instituted, but the looked-for
results did not materialize. The destruction of the traditional means of economic well-being and the concomitant
crushing of Indian political, religious, and social customs
created dispirited communities, which had no motivation
to advance or to succeed.

A Senate select committee appointed in 1880 to inves-
tigate Cheyenne unrest in the Indian Territory declared
that the discontent of the Indians on the reservation to
which they had been forced was a major cause of their
failure to make progress. "If they are compelled to accept
a prison as a home," the committee said, "they will
naturally prefer to compel the keepers to feed and clothe

them. They will remain pensioners upon our humanity, having lost all pride of character and all care of anything except to live."[23]

Among the Sioux the treaty guarantees of goods and services destroyed Indian initiative. James McLaughlin, the agent at Standing Rock, observed in 1882: "They do not wish to cultivate large fields or raise surplus crops, in consequence of which they might be dropped from the ration rolls and obliged to support themselves thereafter."[24] In any case, the Sioux did not take enthusiastically to farming; and the arid lands, the clouds of grasshoppers, and the summer sun and winter blizzards conspired against them.

General George Crook noted a failure to advance among the Sioux with whom he negotiated in 1889 for the reduction of the Great Sioux Reserve in Dakota west of the Missouri River. "When I left you before I expected much good of you," he told the Indians at the Rosebud Reservation, "and here after eleven years I come back and find that you have done but very little towards civilization. You have been contented to sit down and eat rations that the Government gives you, without making any progress, thinking that the Government is always going to keep you. . . . This indolent life you have been living has made squaws of you, and if you don't work and help yourselves you will get such a bad record that the Government will have to send out dolls and rattles to amuse you."[25]

When the anthropologist Margaret Mead studied the Omaha tribe, she depicted the disintegration that had occurred in the attempt to individualize their holdings and thus change the economic system of the tribe. "Never properly accustomed to farming, not yet sufficiently good farmers to make an income very superior [to], or half so reliable as the rent from a white tenant," she wrote, "two-thirds of the Indian men ceased to make any further economic struggle."[26]

In the post–Civil War treaties with their plans for civilization, the benefits to the Indians—schools, food, and other supplies—were promised for limited periods only, because it was assumed that after a generation or so the hoped-for transformation would have occurred and the Indians would be able to provide for themselves. Thus the famous Fort Laramie Treaty of 1868 with the Sioux and other northern-plains tribes declared that the provisions for education would continue for twenty years and that the annuities in the form of clothing and small sums of money would continue for thirty years.[27] But the transformation did not occur, and the federal government was forced to continue its supplies and services.

As education facilities, especially, increased after 1880, the bureaucracy of the Indian Office also greatly expanded, until all aspects of the Indians' lives from cradle to grave seemed to be managed by government officials and employees. The total wardship of the Indians was recognized, but it was thought that when the Indians reached their "majority," the guardian would withdraw his aid and protection, and the Indians would stand on their own.

The government's only solution for the loss of traditional self-sufficiency of the Indians was to change them into small independent farmers or herdsmen. The Indians were expected to cultivate the soil in Anglo-American fashion or to become stock raisers and thus provide sure sustenance for their families. Acquisition and accumulation of goods were to be substituted for reciprocal sharing and generosity. To some extent this had worked with the eastern Indians. The Five Civilized Tribes in Oklahoma—and some others, too—had made the difficult transition. But post–Civil War Indian policy was concerned with the Trans-Mississippi West, and the nomadic Plains Indians were the primary target. These "buffalo Indians" had a different culture from the more sedentary Indians of the East and lived in regions little adapted to 160-acre homesteads. Yet the universal prescription was applied to them. If reduced acreage, a supply of farming equipment, English schools, and Christian missionaries had accomplished their work with the Cherokees and the Choctaws, it was expected that like causes would produce like effects with the Sioux, the Cheyennes, and the Comanches.[28]

The principal means to accomplish the task—aside from formal education—was individualization of reservation lands. The reservations (the sole remaining communal land base of the tribes) were to be allotted in severalty. That is, they were to be divided into 160-acre lots (the traditional area of a white homestead) and distributed to Indian families. With the incentive of a private farm to be cared for, developed, and then bequeathed to one's children, it was assumed that the Indians would enter into the economy and into the social and political life of the nation and thus be assimilated.

After a long legislative struggle the advocates of this "reform" in Indian affairs persuaded Congress to pass the Dawes Severalty Act of 1887. The law authorized the president to survey and allot the reservations; but it also hedged the lands about with restrictions, for the law forbade alienation of the Indian allotments for twenty-five years (a period long enough, it was hoped, to acculturate the Indians to white ways and prevent loss of the lands to white sharpers). As allotments were received and developed, the Indians would once again become self-supporting, their status as wards would end, and the Indian Office would wither away.[29]

The allotment policy was a failure. The Indians, for the most part, did not become self-supporting farmers or ranchers. During the twenty-five-year period the allotments were held in trust by the federal government, and the government, which heretofore had dealt primarily with tribal chiefs, now dealt with thousands upon thousands of individual allottees and entered into the lives of these Indians in a direct way never before envisaged. The allottee was now a ward in a new and more pervasive sense. He could not lease or rent his land without specific permission, could not draw up a will without the Interior Department's approval, and was subject to nearly complete control of his economic life by the "trustee."

In the transition phase between aboriginal economies and the new way of life, government rations and annuities were admitted to be necessary, and they were provided as a temporary expedient. But they were to be a means toward the end, not a perpetual source of subsistence for the Indians. When it became apparent at the turn of the century that the Indians were heavily dependent upon them and were making little effort to provide for themselves, government officials and humanitarian reformers spoke out harshly against the system. Commissioner William A. Jones declared in 1901: "[It has been shown] that the indiscriminate issue of rations was an effectual barrier to civilization; that the periodical distribution of large sums of money was demoralizing in the extreme; and that the general leasing of allotments instead of benefiting the Indians, as originally intended, only contributed to their demoralization." Jones was convinced that the programs had not worked. The Indian, he said, "is still on his reservation; he is still being fed; his children are still being educated and money is still being paid him; he is still dependent upon the Government for existence; mechanics wait on him and farmers still aid him; he is little, if any, nearer the goal of independence than he was thirty years ago, and if the present policy is continued he will get little, if any, nearer in thirty years to come."[30]

Yet there was little change. The government could not simply withdraw its aid and let the Indians founder—although there were a good many persons who urged just that, on the theory that if the Indians hit bottom, they would begin to pull themselves up. So paternalism continued, and with it dependency.

It was these conditions, quite different from what the reformers had intended, that promoted a drive in the second decade of the twentieth century to end the restrictions on Indian land and grant to so-called "competent" Indians full authority over their lands—that is, grant them fee patents that would end government supervision and protection of the land. The theory was that many Indians were unnecessarily remaining dependent upon the federal government as trustee of their property and that they used up resources that might better be spent upon other Indians who still needed protection and guidance (chiefly the Navajos and others in the Southwest). But the granting of patents—euphemistically

called "freeing" the Indians—was no more successful
than the allotments themselves. The criteria for competency (a certain quantum of white blood or graduation
from a government boarding school) were not adequate,
and the competency commissions sent to ferret out competent Indians and set them loose to support themselves
did not accurately appraise the probability of success.[31]

The truth was that many if not most of the allotted
Indians were, in fact, incompetent to handle their own
property, and by 1920 it was clear beyond much doubt
that the so-called "liberal policy" of patenting the Indians
that prevailed during the administration of Woodrow
Wilson was a disaster. Instead of establishing the Indians
as independent property owners and citizens, the policies
pauperized the Indians. The great majority of Indians
who received full control of their land quickly sold the
land or lost it for failure to pay taxes or interest on their
mortgages. The United States Board of Indian Commissioners, which surveyed the effects of the patenting policy in 1921, reported that "the issuance of patents in fee
seems to be a shortcut to the separation of the freed
Indians from their land and cash."[32] Many an Indian who
sold his land used the proceeds to buy an automobile,
but reservation roads were poor and the Indian was not
mechanically inclined so he soon had nothing to show
for his land but a discarded machine.

The economic transformation was supposed to go hand
in hand with a comprehensive national Indian school
system, which would educate the Indians in English letters and train them in vocational skills. Many of these
schools were boarding schools, some off and some on
the reservations, which tore the children away from their

families to immerse them in white civilization. Others were day schools on the reservations. But in all, the goal was to replace Indian ways with white ways, to inculcate the Puritan work ethic, and thus to assimilate the Indians into the mainstream of America. The result—as with the allotment policy—fell short of what was intended. Much of the old culture was destroyed, but the new was not fully accepted, leaving many Indians in a kind of limbo and fostering the spirit of dependency.

The school curriculum was designed by white educators intent on giving the Indian children an education that matched that of white children in the public schools. The objective was self-support, as Estelle Reel, superintendent of Indian schools, declared in 1900: "The Indian must be brought to a point where he will feel the work spirit and become self-supporting, where he will have the ambition to support his family and not look to the Government for help. This point will be reached only through patient application and faithful work along industrial lines."[33]

The schools did not build upon the Indians' own heritage, and much of the curriculum must have made little sense to the Indian pupils. A striking example is a series of examination questions in history administered to the students at the Albuquerque Indian School in 1911. Here are a few examples:

Third grade

> Tell about the voyage of Columbus and why he wanted to go.
> Who were the Pilgrims and where did they land?

Fifth grade

> Why did England tax the colonies? Tell about the "Stamp Act."

Who was Robert Morris?
Name the first three presidents of the United States.

Eighth grade

Explain the difference between the township government of New England and the county government of
Virginia.[34]

It is little wonder that much of the education did not
take, that the Indians continued in a spirit of dependency
that affected so much of their lives.

There was no question, of course, of the Indians'
establishing their own schools. All were provided by the
federal government from congressional appropriations
(except for a number of missionary schools aided by the
trust funds that some tribes had in the Treasury of the
United States). Annual appropriations for Indian schools
showed dramatic increases; the $75,000 provided in 1880
had grown to $2,936,080 in 1900, and to $4,922,325 in
1920.[35] As the twentieth century advanced, more and
more Indian children attended state public schools, but
they too were subsidized there by federal funds because
the Indians paid no taxes for school support. Similarly,
the growing health-care facilities—the physicians, the
nurses, and the hospitals—were supplied by the federal
government.

Many Indians considered that these things were due
them in return for their lands given up to the United
States; they expected them to appear with little effort
on their part. And the goods and services did appear,
for without government aid the continued existence of
the Indians seemed impossible. The psychiatrist Erik H.
Erikson, in his study of the Sioux, said that the Indian
was comparable to what in psychiatry was called a "com-

pensation neurotic," one who received "all his sense of security and identity out of the status of one to whom something is owed."[36]

It is easy to condemn the Indian Office and its friends for the programs that had such disastrous results—dependency instead of self-sufficiency, poverty instead of prosperity, and despondency instead of enthusiasm. But we cannot fault their intentions. They proposed and carried out policies geared to their own experiences, which they in their ethnocentric paternalism knew were best also for the Indians. What they did not understand was that their programs were not well adapted to the Indians' experience and cultural heritage. If the proposals had been applied to white Americans, there would no doubt have been success. Money for investment would have been shrewdly invested, resources would have been skillfully developed, and schooling would have been eagerly sought and quickly absorbed.

We can be helped here by the old principle from scholastic philosophy that was expressed in Latin: *quidquid recipitur, recipitur per modum recipientis*—what is received is received according to the ways of the recipient. Most of the programs did not work with the Indians because the Indians received them with a heritage and cultural outlook that negated or destroyed the well-intentioned plans. A communal rather than an individualistic spirit, an emphasis on sharing rather than on accumulating, a relation with nature that did not accord with rapid exploitation of resources for profit—these traits meant that the seeds of the civilization programs frequently fell on barren ground.

In 1920 the American Indians were still caught in a

complex net of dependency. They had not learned to preserve and exploit their individual property in the white man's world as assimilated citizens. In fact, the better part of their land had passed into white hands. Surplus lands in allotted reservations had been sold to the government for white use; and the allotments themselves (as soon as they were patented) also slipped out of Indian hands. The very land base on which hope for Indian self-sufficiency depended was devastatingly eroded. The Indian Office had not withered away. The Great Father in 1920 was still the guardian of thousands and thousands of dependent Indian wards.

3
Indian Rights

The paternalism that marked American Indian policy was not an end in itself (even though it might be argued that the bureaucracy in which the paternalism was embodied tended to perpetuate itself). The goal of the benevolent humanitarians who had such great influence on Indian policy in the nineteenth century was assimilation of the Indians into the general American citizenry. The solution to dependency/paternalism was seen to be the vanishing of the Indians by absorption into the dominant white Christian society of the nation. When the Indians were thus assimilated, reformers repeated again and again, there would be no "Indian problem" because there would no longer be any Indians. The Indian Bureau, charged with care of the Indians through its varied programs, would then disappear.

In the nineteenth century and the first two decades of the twentieth, this movement to acculturate, assimilate, and Americanize the Indians was the single force dominating federal Indian affairs. There were only a few nay-sayers, a mere handful of perceptive men who saw that it would be difficult if not impossible to achieve the goals of the assimilationists. On the part of the Indians there were varied responses—withdrawal, armed resistance, passivity—but in the end the tribesmen were subordinated to the power of the United States. The result was the pervasive paternalism and the almost absolute dependency that we have already examined.

The period after 1920, in contradistinction, was marked by a duality of purpose on the part of the dominant society—an ambivalence, if you will, about the proper destiny of the Indians in American society and about the policy that the government should follow. Two patterns of thought struggled for dominance, sometimes in overt and conscious conflict, sometimes, it seems, without the actors themselves being aware of them. At times one gained ascendancy in the public councils of the nation, at different times the other, but neither was able to hold the field absolutely. The result was a collection of wonderfully paradoxical circumstances that continue to our own time.

There was first of all, and understandably enough, a strong residue of the assimilationist philosophy. Committed reformers lived on, in the Indian Rights Association and the Board of Indian Commissioners, for example; the idea that alien groups with special restrictions or special privileges did not belong in America never died out completely.

But, second, there was also a new philosophy of "Indian reform," one that sought protection, preservation, and strengthening of Indian ways in art, religion, and social organization. This philosophy offered an alternative answer to Indian dependency: reconstitution and strengthening of Indian tribes in some sort of autonomy, self-sufficiency, semisovereignty, or self-determination. The Indians would then return to a status comparable to what they had lost when the Europeans invaded the New World, albeit within the context of ultimate United States sovereignty. If the Indians, with reconstituted tribal governments, could develop self-sufficient economies on their reservations, strengthen or recover their cultural patterns, and deal with the United States government and the white population again as equal brothers in a pluralistic society, not as dependent children or wards, the whole syndrome of paternalism could be eliminated.

The nineteenth-century answer had failed. The Indians had not been assimilated as individual yeoman farmers or stockmen; they were not able (by and large) to profit from private ownership of allotted sections of the old reservations. They were not served effectively by social services provided by the states for white citizens.

After 1920 these failures were recognized by a new group of reformers, who sought to rehabilitate the Indians economically and spiritually. There was, in fact, a strong and significantly successful movement to restore pride in their heritage to the Indians and to create respect for the Indian heritage on the part of whites. Allotment was ended, and attempts were made to preserve and augment Indian tribal landholdings. Reestablishment of tribal governments and encouragement of tribal corporate economic activity became prominent goals.

The place of Indians in American society thus underwent a transformation that could hardly have been envisaged by the assimilationists of earlier decades. The Indians, who were supposed to be a vanishing race, made a remarkable comeback. Indian population, according to the federal census, was only 237,196 in 1900. Then, because of the increasing concern for health and sanitation, it slowly started to climb upward. By 1920 the census enumerated 244,437 Indians, and at mid-century, 357,499.[1]

At the same time appeared a significant shift in public

opinion about the value and importance of Indian cultures. The old view that Indian cultures had nothing to offer American society, that the sooner they were destroyed and replaced the better, gave way little by little to an interest in Indian ways and then to a positive appreciation of Indian art and other contributions. In part this came from a new scientific outlook, which argued that diverse cultures should be studied and evaluated on their own terms, not measured by the norms of the dominant white society. In part it was simply a belated recognition by government officials of the noble qualities of the Indians with whom they came in contact, qualities that had not been crushed by the tremendous cultural assault of the assimilationists and that should be fostered and preserved.

There were some initial indications of the new outlook even before 1920. Most notable were the views of Francis E. Leupp, commissioner of Indian affairs during Theodore Roosevelt's second term. Leupp crossed swords with the Christian reformers, whom he did not want meddling in his running of the Indian Office; and although he saw the need for Indians to acquire skills that would enable them to be self-supporting in twentieth-century America, he admired Indian traits of character. "The Indian is a natural warrior, a natural logician, a natural artist," he asserted in 1905. "We have room for all three in our highly organized social system. Let us not make the mistake, in the process of absorbing them, of washing out of them whatever is distinctly Indian. Our aboriginal brother brings, as his contribution to the common store of character, a great deal that is admirable, and which needs only to be developed along the right line. Our proper work with him is improvement, not transformation." Leupp wanted to preserve and cultivate Indian art and music, not eradicate them, and he refused to assume that the Indian was "simply a white man with a red skin."[2]

The new acceptance of a sort of pluralism, the rejection of the demand for absolute conformity to the worldview and mores of white America, came primarily with the collapse of the Protestant hegemony. The concept of a "Christian America" (the context in which the evangelical reformers had worked) faded by the 1920s. The postwar period saw a strong reaction against idealism and reform, a condition growing out of the disillusionment with American participation in World War I. But, beyond that, the very life of the nation had changed from what it had been in prewar days, for evangelical Protestantism was being displaced as the "primary definer of cultural values and behavior patterns in the nation." The belief that the United States as a nation was basically Protestant and that it was progressing toward the kingdom of God had supported evangelical crusading, and the crusade for Americanizing the Indians in this mold was no exception. But in the 1920s the old supports were crumbling.[3]

A new secularization of society appeared that was uncongenial to religion. Doctrines of social freedom eroded the old ways, and the bitter controversy between fundamentalists and modernists further lessened the prestige of Protestantism. More basic than anything else were the new advances in science and technology that bred a devotion to scientific method and led to disillusionment with religion. There was a growing optimism that science could solve all human problems, and the belief that progress depended upon religion was irreparably weakened.

Concern for the Indians underwent a marked shift in keeping with the changes in American society. The old philanthropic, benevolent approach, which saw as the highest good for the Indians the absolute imitation of their white Christian advisers, was challenged by a social science approach that aimed at cultural understanding and at a secular solution to Indian problems. It was the anthropologist now, not the missionary, who was at the cutting edge of Indian-policy reform.

In the 1920s came a concerted drive to preserve Indian culture and to protect Indian rights. This was the work primarily of a remarkable social reformer named John Collier, who had worked among the immigrants of New York City and who had a dream of a new society based on communal spirit, not on the individual competition that marked the industrial age. In 1920 on a trip to the Southwest, Collier encountered the Pueblo Indians. In them he thought he had discovered the very sort of society he had seen in his visions. When the Pueblos were threatened in 1922 by legislation that would have transferred rights to large parts of their traditional lands to whites, Collier led a national crusade to protect the Pueblos' land and by extension their culture and that of all the Indians of the nation. For the next two decades and more, Collier was the dominant figure in American Indian affairs; he ultimately worked a revolution in Indian policy.[4]

Collier was a scrappy and aggressive fighter for Indian rights. He organized an All Pueblo Council to protest the land changes. He established the American Indian Defense Association, a group of white supporters that became a dominant force in protesting the old policy and instituting a new one. Wherever there was a threat to

Indian culture or property rights, Collier led a march to counteract it, aiming his attack chiefly at the officials in the Bureau of Indian Affairs, whom he considered holdovers from the old and indefensible policy of allotment of lands and forced assimilation.

A typical Collier caper, rich in symbolic significance, was his attack beginning in 1923 on the government's attempt (supported by old-line Christian reformers such as those in the Indian Rights Association) to suppress Indian dances and religious ceremonies. The critics of the Indian customs, of whom Commissioner of Indian Affairs Charles H. Burke was the chief spokesman, had two lines of objection. At first they were concerned chiefly with the deleterious effect that time-consuming dances had on Indian efforts at farming, but the second charge soon overshadowed the first. It was the accusation that the Indian ceremonies (especially in the Southwest) were obscene spectacles that needed to be stamped out.[5]

This attack on Indian culture infuriated John Collier. Whereas the Bureau of Indian Affairs and the Indian Rights Association saw immorality and degradation in the ceremonies, Collier saw beauty and mystical experience. Here was a striking example of the conflict between the old and the new in Indian policy, between the Christian missionary influence and the growing power of a secular and social science approach. Although the former continued to exist in American society, never again was it possible simply to condemn and suppress Indian ways; little by little, administrative, legislative, and court action gave protection to Indian religious beliefs and practices.

For a decade John Collier was a gadfly, an articulate critic of the Indian Bureau and its adherence to the old policy and outlook. He was aided at the end of the 1920s by a sober, scientific appraisal of Indian affairs made by the independent Institute for Government Research under the direction of Lewis Meriam. The report issued in February 1928, officially called *The Problem of Indian Administration* but usually referred to as the Meriam Report, was a searching and constructive critique of how Indian affairs had been handled by the federal government. Although not a manifesto in support of Indian rights—it was at heart a plea for more effective administration of the traditional programs for the Indians in education, health, and economic development—the report stirred up new concern for Indians and gave support to those who advocated substantial change.[6]

President Herbert Hoover, who soon came into office, appointed two Quakers to run the Indian Bureau— Charles J. Rhoads and J. Henry Scattergood—and they took the Meriam Report as their blueprint. Collier at first was pleased with the appointments and worked with the Interior Department on a series of proposals to benefit the Indians. But the new administration was too cautious and reform came too slowly to satisfy Collier, who soon renewed his attacks on the Indian Bureau.[7]

The culmination of Collier's efforts came with the New Deal of Franklin Delano Roosevelt, for Roosevelt appointed Collier commissioner of Indian affairs. The untiring critic was then in a position to push forward his own design for the Indians in American society. He began an "Indian New Deal" that had significant and irreversible effects on the development of Indian communities in the United States.[8]

Collier believed that Indian societies could be regenerated and given substantial responsibility and power. He insisted that land be held and used in the way each Indian group desired and that cultural and religious liberty be guaranteed. Most of all he wanted for the Indians "the experience of responsible democracy" as self-governing, self-determining entities.[9]

Collier submitted a legislative proposal to Congress that embodied his radical policies. This proposal, introduced as the Wheeler-Howard bill, in its original form would have reestablished tribal lands by authorizing the secretary of the interior to transfer individual land interests to the tribe and by directing that on the death of an allottee his restricted lands would pass not to his heirs but to the chartered community or tribe, and it would have given tribal governments extensive powers over political and economic life. The Indians, many of whom were already deeply involved in an individualistic society with their private property and who participated in white governmental procedures, were hesitant about accepting this new plan emanating from Washington. Collier, however, was insistent, and he took his proposals to the Indians, called to meet in congresses around the country. Here he and his lieutenants patiently explained the bill and listened to the Indian criticisms. White reform organizations, too, whom Collier thought he had firmly in his camp, began to question the wisdom of a return to tribalism (a reversal of their long-cherished vision for the Indian's destiny).

Collier retreated and offered amendments to the bill to meet the most adamant critics, but the bill, passed on June 18, 1934, as the Indian Reorganization Act, incorporated fundamental provisions for political self-government and economic self-determination. Indian tribes could draw up constitutions and bylaws for a tribal government—consisting principally of an elected tribal council and tribal chairman. They could incorporate for purposes of economic development, and a revolving credit fund provided money for business ventures. Allotment of lands ended, the trust period for tribal and individual lands was indefinitely extended, and money was authorized to purchase additional lands. There were provisions for vocational education and authority for preferential employment of Indians in the Bureau of Indian Affairs.[10] Tribes were permitted to vote on whether or not they wished to come under the law.

Even though acceptance of the Indian Reorganization Act was by no means universal (for example, the largest of the tribes, the Navajos, voted to reject it), the legislation was a dramatic event. Collier exclaimed, "One becomes a little breathless when one realizes that the Allotment Law—the agony and ruin of the Indians—has been repealed." And he rightly noted that any single part of the law by itself would have been an important change in government policy.[11] Moreover, Collier was able by administrative measures to push forward elements of his original plans that had been eliminated in the congressional legislation, and there was supplementary legislation, too, such as the Indian Arts and Crafts Act of 1935, which promoted the production and marketing of Indian crafts both as a contribution to American life and as an economic benefit to poverty-stricken tribes, and the extension of many of the provisions of the Indian Reorganization Act to Oklahoma Indians, who had been excluded from the law, and to Alaska Natives.

Collier was an astute propagandist for his own positions, and for many years his view of the Indian New

Deal was accepted as the proper historical account. He reported that there had been a sharp and successful reversal of policy, that the individualizing and assimilationist philosophy associated with the Dawes Act had been replaced by a forward-looking policy of Indian self-determination and tribal resurgence. To him it seemed that the assimilationists had been routed and Indian self-determination firmly established.

Today's historians are more cautious. The Indian Reorganization Act and its concomitant reform legislation, it must be admitted, had major flaws. In the first place, Collier's deepest personal experience with Indians was with the Pueblos of the Southwest, the Indian communities that had been least affected by Anglo-American culture and that had therefore maintained intact large elements of their political, religious, and social structures. A continuation or rebuilding of tribal ways was possible with them because so much still existed. But for many other tribes the incursion of assimilationist forces had gone too far to be reversed, and acculturated Indians refused to accept Collier's invitation to turn the clock back. Moreover, Collier's concern for necessary economic programs for the Indians led him to organize the Indians on a tribal basis, when in fact traditional Indian economic units in many cases were not the tribe but the smaller units of the band or village.[12]

More damaging is the accusation that an alien form of tribal government was imposed on the tribes by the constitutions adopted under the Indian Reorganization Act. Although Collier insisted that each tribe had been allowed to draw up its own constitution, as a matter of fact most of them simply adopted (with minor adaptations) the model form supplied by the Bureau of Indian Affairs. These tribal governments, with councils and tribal chairmen elected by majority vote, were Anglo-American inventions, which did not accord with traditional Indian ways. Many traditional spiritual leaders of the tribes today and their adherents consider the Indian Reorganization Act governments as subservient to the Bureau of Indian Affairs and speak of the incumbents as "BIA Indians." Collier, in his sincere attempt to restore Indian self-government and self-determination, may well have saddled tribes with forms of government and forms of economic organization that did not really fit. His actions could be viewed—as some Indians did indeed view them—as particularly crass instances of continuing government paternalism.

The Indian Reorganization Act, it is true, did contain strong paternalistic elements in the heavy federal supervision of the Indians that it directed. The law gave the initiative to the secretary of the interior for carrying out the law or required his approval of Indian actions. Even a partial listing of the authority given the secretary shows the abiding federal influence in tribal matters: to sell or transfer tribal lands; to purchase lands for tribal use; to proclaim new Indian reservations; to make rules and regulations for management of Indian ranges and forests; to spend appropriated funds to defray the expenses of organizing Indian corporations; to make loans from the revolving credit fund; to establish standards for employment of Indians outside of civil-service rules; to call elections for voting on acceptance of the Indian Reorganization Act; to establish rules for elections to ratify constitutions; to approve legal counsel engaged by the tribes; and to charter Indian corporations.

The present-day Indian writer Vine Deloria, Jr., reports the frequent charge that the Bureau of Indian Affairs "set up puppet governments on the reservations and somehow mysteriously governs all aspects of tribal life by remote control."[13]

Collier did not always have easy sailing with his new Indian policy. There were strong elements in Congress and among some Indian groups, too, that continued to hold firm to assimilationist principles and refused to sanction what some considered a return to tribalism and paganism. As the years passed, Collier and his program encountered strenuous opposition from Congress. Finally, in 1945, Collier, hoping that increased appropriations might come for Indian affairs if the bureau were headed by a less controversial figure than himself, resigned.

The paradoxical elements of the Indian New Deal should not obscure the important legacy of Collier. He revitalized Indian communities that were economically depressed and spiritually crushed. He himself saw the aim of the Indian Reorganization Act as twofold: first, economic rehabilitation, through overthrow of the allotment system and establishment of credit facilities to stimulate economic development, but second, "spiritual rehabilitation." Under the old policies, Collier asserted, "the Indians have been robbed of initiative, their spirit has been broken, their health undermined, and their native pride ground into the dust." He saw the Indian Reorganization Act as a "means of destroying this inferiority complex," of sustaining the "awakening of the racial spirit," and of enabling the Indians, "after a century of spoliation, suppression, and paternalism," to learn again how to manage their own affairs.[14]

Collier was followed by a brief but crucial period in which many of the goals he had fought for were set aside as an aberration, a period in which the old assimilationist philosophy once more became a dominant force. The new movement sought to "free the Indians." The freedom was to release the Indians from the overriding guardianship of the federal government, which would terminate its responsibility to protect and provide services for those tribal groups judged ready and able to fend for themselves. Termination, to use the accepted designation of the new policy, was fundamentally a drive to undo the basic policies of Collier.

Yet we cannot look at the change as a matter of black and white. Although termination came to be thought of as a single principle that lined up promoters against opponents, in fact there were many ambiguities. The repeal of discriminatory legislation was sought by Indians and their friends and was, in fact, a continuation of action inaugurated by Collier. Transfer of some services for Indians—education, health, and welfare—to other federal agencies or to the states had been an important ingredient of the Indian New Deal. The concept of a special claims commission to handle Indian claims against the government, which had been advocated by Collier but not established by Congress until 1946, became tied in with terminationist philosophy. *Freedom* and *emancipation* resonated with both Collier's policies of self-determination and the insistence of Indian New Deal critics that the Indian Bureau be abolished. Thus there came together in the termination policy of the 1950s a good many threads of history, not only from the assimilationist era of the nineteenth and early twentieth centuries but from the reform movement of the 1920s and 1930s as well.[15]

Although there was a kind of inner dynamism within the movement that came from a firmly held philosophical position that the Indians must be integrated into white society and not be allowed or encouraged to remain a segregated segment within the nation, the termination era coincided with and was strengthened by the political and economic conditions of the decade. Postwar economy moves called for reduction of government spending. The period was a time of economic growth, and the tying up of Indian lands and other resources in tribal enclaves went against the prevailing mood. The Cold War between the United States and the Soviet Union placed particular value on national unity and conformity, and special groups, especially if they emphasized communal values, were considered out of line. And as the growing population pushed beyond the capabilities of the reservations to support it, a movement to urban centers, with consequent assimilationist pressures, coincided with the termination actions of the government.

The leading promoter of termination was Senator Arthur V. Watkins of Utah, who looked upon the Indian New Deal as a serious mistake. Watkins wrote in 1957: "Unfortunately, the major and continuing Congressional movement toward full freedom was delayed for a time by the Indian Reorganization Act of 1934, the Wheeler-Howard Act. Amid the deep social concern of the depression years, Congress deviated from its accustomed policy under the concept of promoting the general Indian welfare. In the post-depression years Congress—realizing this change of policy—sought to return to the historic

principles of much earlier decades." He issued a stirring
cry for action: "Firm and constant consideration for those
of Indian ancestry should lead us all to work diligently
and carefully for the full realization of their national
citizenship with all other Americans. Following in the
footsteps of the Emancipation Proclamation of ninety-
four years ago, I see the following words emblazoned in
letters of fire above the heads of the Indians—*THESE
PEOPLE SHALL BE FREE!*"[16]

Congress issued a joint resolution in 1953 declaring it
to be the intent of Congress to free Indians "from Federal
supervision and control and from all disabilities and limitations specially applicable to Indians."[17] The Bureau of
Indian Affairs, under Commissioner Dillon S. Myer,
accepting the congressional initiative, surveyed the reservations to prepare for terminating the tribes. And in the
mid-1950s a number of termination laws were passed,
notably for the Menominee Indians of Wisconsin and the
Klamath Indians of Oregon. When these laws went into
effect, the federal government gave up its trusteeship of
the Indians' property, all federal services for the Indians
(education and health care especially) ceased, and the
Indians were thrown upon their own resources and those
of the states in which they lived. There was to be no
more federal paternalism for the terminated tribes, no
more dependency upon the Great Father in Washington.

A concomitant policy in the 1950s was the relocation
of Indians from the overcrowded reservations to urban
areas where employment opportunities might be greater.
Relocation centers were established in cities like Los
Angeles, Chicago, and Detroit to assist the Indians in the
difficult transition from reservation to city life. And
thousands of Indians, without federal encouragement or

aid, pushed simply by economic or social pressures, joined the migration. The Indians in the cities, once relocated, were generally beyond the concern of the Bureau of Indian Affairs, which looked primarily to reservation Indians, so urbanization appeared to be another way to cut federal ties with Indians.[18]

But most Indians were not ready or prepared to cut their ties to the federal government on which they had for so long come to depend. As soon as the full realization of what termination meant struck the Indians—that the federal government would no longer protect and supervise their property as trustee, that the federal Indian programs would end, that Indians would have to pay taxes for support of their schools and hospitals, that they would be forced to run their businesses in competition with more modernized rivals—cries of anguish and anger filled the air.

Here was another great paradox. Indian leaders and Indian organizations, using the skills and experience gained under the programs of the Indian New Deal and energized by the respiriting of their Indian pride that had been Collier's great contribution, demanded a continuation of the paternal role of the federal government in their lives. They were not yet ready to operate without the federal support systems.

The Indian agitation, augmented by white activism, was successful in halting the termination drive. Only three percent of the total Indian population was terminated, and the same percentage of Indian lands was removed from federal trust status. One might well wonder then why so much attention has been paid to termination.

The answer lies in the psychological effect upon the Indian communities, the almost paralyzing fear that Congress would terminate the federal responsibility toward them and set them adrift. Every administrative or legislative measure touching Indians was scrutinized by the Indians and their attorneys to see if there were any hidden elements of termination. Proposals to turn over Indian programs to the Indians themselves or to the states were especially suspected of being termination measures in disguise. No Indian group wanted to do too much on its own lest its actions be interpreted as a readiness for the withdrawal of federal services.

So, although termination was quickly seen as unworkable and condemned by responsible federal officials, the fact that it had occurred was indication enough that the assimilationist force in Indian affairs was by no means completely moribund. It lurked below the surface, ready to spring forth again, the Indians feared, if ever they gave up their active vigilance against the danger.

But if termination of the Indian tribes was not an acceptable policy for dealing with the Indians in American society, what should be substituted for it? Certainly, the old wardship and paternalism, whose limitations had been recognized and whose continuation had been loudly denounced for many years, could not intentionally be reconstituted. Was there some middle ground between the thrust of complete assimilation that marked the termination policy and the insufferable dependency that marked the wardship of the Indians in the early decades of the twentieth century?

The officials of the federal government in the decade of the 1960s thought they had found it in economic development of the reservations. Economic development, of course, was an old song, going back thirty years

at least to the heyday of John Collier's Indian New Deal
with its provisions for chartered tribal corporations and
revolving funds to supply needed credit. But the sixties
brought a new realization that the promises of the New
Deal (and the Indian New Deal was part of that event)
had not been fully realized in America. Beginning with
President John F. Kennedy and reaching a full swell
under Lyndon B. Johnson came a war on poverty that
would in the end produce the Great Society. As they had
always been, the Indians were caught up in the movements that stirred American society as a whole.[19]

The economic development, however, was not to be
masterminded solely by the Bureau of Indian Affairs.
The new watchword was "Indian participation," and evi-
dences of the new spirit were plentiful at the beginning
of the 1960s, from both inside and outside the government. The decade began with significant statements of
what the future should bring for the Indians. One was
the 1961 report of an independent study group supported
by the Fund for the Republic, with the impressive title
Commission on the Rights, Liberties, and Responsibilities of the American Indian. The commission condemned
the termination policy of the 1950s and insisted that
programs for Indians should not be imposed from above
but should be based on the initiative of the Indians themselves and carried out with their intelligent cooperation.
The commission spoke of the "bounden duty" of the
United States to assist the Indians in progressing "from
the present poverty to a decent standard of living" and
made recommendations about tribal government, education programs, and Indian health services.[20]

A second event was the American Indian Chicago
Conference, held at the University of Chicago in June

1961, at which more than 450 Indian delegates from ninety tribes met for a week to discuss problems and proposals. In a formal Declaration of Indian Purpose the meeting called for an end of the "so-called termination policy of the last administration" and urged economic assistance to tribes with full Indian participation in development programs. "What we ask of America," the declaration concluded, "is not charity, nor paternalism, even when benevolent. We ask only that the nature of our situation be recognized and made the basis of policy and action. In short, the Indians ask for assistance, technical and financial, for the time needed, however long that may be, to regain in the America of the space age some measure of the adjustment they enjoyed as the original possessors of their native land."[21]

The third report, and the most important because it became the basis for official policy, was that of the Task Force on Indian Affairs, appointed by Kennedy's secretary of the interior, Stewart Udall. Like the other reports, this one rejected termination and called for development of the reservations. "What we are attempting to do for those in the underdeveloped areas of the world," it said, "we can and must also do for the Indians here at home. Furthermore," it added, "to insure the success of our endeavor we must solicit the collaboration of those whom we hope to benefit—the Indians themselves. To do otherwise is contrary to the American concept of democracy." The Task Force spoke of a "new trail" for the Indians, one that led to "equal citizenship, maximum self-sufficiency, and full participation in American life."[22]

These were not merely empty slogans. Philleo Nash, a member of the Task Force who was appointed commissioner of Indian affairs, worked with tribal leaders, civic organizations, and industrial groups to promote industrial development on or near reservations and established a new Division of Economic Development within the BIA. Such efforts were aided greatly by the Office of Economic Opportunity, the result of Johnson's war on poverty. Indians and Indian communities participated broadly in the OEO programs, especially the community action programs. The funds provided were significant, but more important was the boost given to Indian management of the various programs.[23]

The drive toward Indian self-determination continued under Nash's successor, the Oneida Indian Robert L. Bennett, with whom was initiated the continuing policy that the commissionership and other high-level administrative offices dealing with Indian affairs be filled by Indians, not whites. Bennett spoke grandly of a new era in federal-Indian relations, "an era in which the expressed wishes and hope of all Indians will be fulfilled through their own active participation in the making of policy and law." And he added the now-expected condemnation of paternalism. "Paternalism and its stifling effects . . . ," he declared, "should be eliminated. Paternalism creates attitudes of dependency which restrains the social and economic advancement of Indian people. As I see it, the Congress and the Bureau must bring about a real, genuine, partnership with Indian leadership."[24]

Bennett supported the development programs of his predecessors, and he was encouraged by President Johnson's special message to Congress on the problems of the American Indian, "The Forgotten American," in March 1968, in which the president proposed "a new goal for our Indian programs: a goal that ends the

old debate about 'termination' of Indian programs and
stresses self-determination, a goal that erases the attitudes of paternalism and promotes partnership self-help."
Johnson asked for more funds for Indian programs and
created a White House–based National Council on Indian
Opportunity to coordinate efforts for Indian welfare.[25]

But the old attitudes of paternalism could not be erased
as easily as Johnson assumed. In large part this was due
to the inordinate and continuing fear on the part of the
Indians that independence and self-determination on their
part would be interpreted as a step toward termination.
When Secretary Udall in 1967 promoted an Indian Resources Development Act, a measure he called "the most
important legislation proposed for American Indians
since the Wheeler-Howard Act of 1934," Indians raised
strong objections because they feared it would lead to
termination, and the bill failed. In 1969 Commissioner
Bennett candidly admitted, "Positive attempts to bring
about the development of the Indian people . . . meet
with outright suspicion by the Indians." And at the end
of his administration he noted that long-standing problems of economic advance for the Indians had little pros-
pect of immediate solution.[26]

In the matter of civil rights for Indians, the 1960s
ended with a remarkable instance of the strange interplay
between recognition of the equality of Indians in American society and simultaneous recognition of Indian autonomy and self-determination that has become the
hallmark of modern Indian-white relations. This was the
Civil Rights Act of 1968, which besides its general pro-
motion of civil rights in Title I included five titles dealing
with the Indians.[27]

The law was the work of Senator Sam J. Ervin, Jr., of North Carolina, who was obsessed with the conviction that Indians living on reservations under tribal governments should have a system of justice that insured the constitutional rights which apply to all citizens of the United States. Ervin wanted simply to subject Indian tribal governments to the limitations set on the federal government and the state governments by the Bill of Rights and the Fourteenth Amendment. It soon became clear from the testimony of Indian leaders and government officials, however, that this was too sweeping a limitation. Tribal government had unique characteristics, and application of the full Bill of Rights to them would upset traditional governing practices. Especially crucial was the prohibition against the "establishment of religion," which would have obstructed the quasi-theocracies that ran some Indian communities. In the end, the blanket extension of the Bill of Rights to tribal governments was replaced by a selective and specific list of individual rights to be protected. The law, furthermore, specifically authorized the writ of habeas corpus in federal courts for persons detained by order of an Indian tribe, and restrictions were placed on the assumption of jurisdiction by states over Indian reservations.

The mixed reception accorded the Indian Civil Rights Act indicated the tension between assimilationists and self-determinationists, between congressional intent to protect the rights of individual Indians and the stated policy of fostering tribal self-government. The Indians, of whom the Pueblos of New Mexico were most outspoken, were concerned about the application of United States legal forms to tribal governments and what this might do to self-government and tribal sovereignty.

Cases were accepted by federal courts to enforce the Indian bill of rights in such matters as tribal membership, tribal elections, and selection of tribal officers; the decisions were seen by critics of the act as intrusions upon the self-government of the tribes.[28]

Much of the tension was eased by the case of *Santa Clara Pueblo* v. *Martinez* in 1978, in which the Supreme Court declared that suits against the tribe under the Civil Rights Act were barred by the tribe's sovereign immunity to suit. The court noted that the act had two distinct purposes: to protect individual tribal members from violation of their civil rights by the tribe, but also to promote "the well-established federal policy" of encouraging self-government. "Creation of a federal cause of action for the enforcement of the rights [in the act] . . . plainly would be at odds with the congressional goal of protecting tribal self government," the court ruled. "Not only would it undermine the authority of tribal forums . . . but it would also impose serious financial burdens on already 'financially disadvantaged' tribes."[29] Thus the ultimate interpretation of the legislation supported tribal autonomy, but at the cost, some analysts maintained, of failing to protect individual rights from tribal authority.

The "new trail" promoted by the Task Force on Indian Affairs in 1961 had by the end of the decade led the Indians a considerable distance toward the goal of self-determination they envisaged. Building on the spirit and the mechanisms embedded in Collier's Indian New Deal and banding together in a new pan-Indianism to prevent the recurrence of forced and disastrous termination of federal responsibility, Indians were ready to demand of American society redress of past wrongs, an important place in the consciousness of the American public, and official recognition of tribal sovereignty. Henry L. Dawes and Thomas Jefferson Morgan would have stared in disbelief, and even John Collier would have been surprised.

4
Self-Determination

Recent years have in many ways been the most exciting and most fruitful period in the history of Indian relations in the United States. The movement toward self-determination, which began in the 1920s and 1930s with John Collier's crusade for Indian reform and which advanced so rapidly in the 1960s after the brief hiatus of termination, reached a high point in the 1970s. For some people—a majority perhaps of Americans—Indians are still a romantic topic. Iconographic symbols of Indians that everyone recognizes all come out of the past—bows and arrows, smoke signals, tomahawks, peace pipes, long braids, fringed buckskin shirts, feathered headdresses, beaded moccasins, and tepees. Indians themselves often play upon some of these attributes in order to be considered unmistakably Indian. But these residues of an earlier material culture, which no doubt are useful in maintaining the Indians' pride in their heritage, should not obscure the reality of Indian existence in the last quarter of the twentieth century.[1]

The organization of tribal governments, the legal skills developed during the proceedings before the Indian Claims Commission, the movement toward pan-Indian activity, and an increasing sophistication in handling tribal business and in dealing with the federal government all have contributed to a new reality in today's

Indian affairs. Peter MacDonald, who from 1970 to 1982 was chairman of the Navajo Nation, in his trim business suit conducting the deliberations of the Navajo Tribal Council in its modern tribal headquarters building, is a much better symbol of the Indian in contemporary society than Sitting Bull or Crazy Horse (who still get the public's attention).[2] The Indians today seek to protect their tribal autonomy and Indian heritage by skillful use of Anglo-American forms and agencies, while at the same time they promote the revival of tribal sovereignty. Traditional ways, of course, have by no means disappeared. To an amazing extent, considering the assault on their customs by the assimilationists over the years, many Indians have preserved much of their culture, and in the new era of respect for their rights and dignity, the Indians' spiritual values and social arrangements have blossomed again.

Indians have learned, and learned well, the tactics of confrontation. Seizures of government or private property and other obstructive actions became media events and effectively placed the Indians' "plight" before the television viewers and newspaper readers of the nation and to some extent of the world. And Indian activists exploited the events to great advantage. Americans in the 1970s could no longer be unaware that Indians were still part of the American scene.[3]

The seizure in 1969 of Alcatraz Island in San Francisco Bay—the abandoned federal high-security penitentiary—by a varied group of young Indians who called themselves Indians of All Tribes was an effective beginning. Facetiously offering to buy the island for twenty-four dollars' worth of beads, the Indians demanded that Alcatraz be turned into an Indian cultural and educational center. The federal government rejected these proposals, offering instead to make the island a national park with an Indian theme and Indian employees, but the occupiers held fast to their original demands. The community of Indians on Alcatraz was visited by thousands of well-wishers and drew support from many tribes and many white sympathizers; yet it could not maintain itself and eventually, under pressure from the government, evacuated the island.[4]

Then, just before the national presidential election in November 1972, a caravan of Indian protesters invaded Washington, D.C., with twenty demands in their pocket for a reinstatement of tribal sovereignty and enforcement of treaty rights. It called itself the Trail of Broken Treaties and was organized by a group known as the American Indian Movement (AIM). Frustrated by their cool reception from federal officialdom and by inadequate provisions for housing, the Indians seized the Bureau of Indian Affairs headquarters building on Constitution Avenue. With a large sign flying over the entrance proclaiming the American Indian Embassy, the Indians refused to be dislodged. When they were threatened with forcible removal, they destroyed the interior of the building in a fit of anger and desperation. At length they were persuaded to leave (with money provided for the return trip from federal funds), but the force of the demonstration frightened government officials. The BIA was dispersed and reorganized, and Congress investigated possible foreign influence in AIM. No one any longer doubted that Indian conditions were serious enough to lead to violence.[5]

AIM's determination to electrify the nation next found an outlet in the seizure of the village of Wounded Knee on the Pine Ridge Indian Reservation in South Dakota. The site of the fatal confrontation of Indian ghost dancers and the United States Seventh Cavalry in 1890, Wounded Knee had also become a household word as a result of Dee Brown's best-selling *Bury My Heart at Wounded Knee,* published in 1971. In a lengthy standoff with the FBI that threatened to turn into a bloodbath, the Indians staged effective media presentations that again captured the attention of the nation. The denouement was less dramatic than the original confrontation, but the memory lingered on.[6]

None of the seizures accomplished what was intended. But they made it clear that the Indians' situation needed serious attention and that militant Indians were not going to let the country rest until remedies were found. It was within this atmosphere of tension and concern that reasonable people worked toward positive accomplishments of great moment.

Much of the advance came in the presidency of Richard M. Nixon, who wanted Indian self-determination to be taken seriously. He stated his principles forthrightly during his election campaign: "Termination of tribal recognition will not be a policy objective and in no case will it be imposed without Indian consent. . . . The right of self-determination of the Indian people will be respected and their participation in planning their own destiny will actively be encouraged." In 1970 Nixon sent a special message to Congress on Indian affairs that formally restated this position. In a phrase that became the slogan of his Indian policy, Nixon called for self-determination without termination, thus rejecting two extremes—federal termination on the one hand and federal paternalism on the other. His goal, he said, was "to strengthen the Indian's sense of autonomy without threatening his sense of community." "We must make it clear," he concluded, "that Indians can become independent of Federal control without being cut off from Federal concern and Federal support."[7]

Early in his administration came three important pieces of legislation, which not only were practical measures of importance but also were of high symbolic value in marking the "new era" that Nixon called for.

The first of these was the return of the sacred Blue Lake to Taos Pueblo in New Mexico. The lake and the surrounding forests had been taken from the Indians by President Theodore Roosevelt in 1906 and added to Carson National Forest. The Indians insisted that the region was sacred to them and necessary for important religious rites, and they fought over the years to regain exclusive control of the lake and the forests. On December 15, 1970, Nixon signed a bill returning Blue Lake and forty-eight thousand acres of land to Taos. The president noted that this was not a gift to the Indians but the returning of what was rightfully theirs, and that the law involved respect for the Indians' religion. "We restore this place of worship to them," Nixon said, "for all years to come."[8]

Another signal event was the settlement in 1971 of the land claims of Alaska Natives, a recognition of native claims to the resources of the region that had been unresolved ever since the United States acquired Alaska in 1867. There were conflicting views among the new state of Alaska, the federal government, and the Alaska Natives about what was a just and equitable settlement, but in the end it was the proposal of the Alaska Native Federation that prevailed. The Alaska Native Claims Settlement Act of December 18, 1971, granted the natives legal title to forty million acres and provided compensation of nearly one billion dollars. Village and regional corporations of Alaska Natives were established to manage the assets. "After more than four hundred years," a noted Indian scholar wrote after the passage of the act, "a native people and a colonizing power had come to terms. What had been expressed as a piety by Spanish humanists, then elevated into law in British North America, had met the harsh test of the market. The Natives of Alaska had asserted their rights as original owners of the soil—rights which priests, statesmen, and jurists had recognized, and frontier society had largely ignored—and their claim had been honored."[9]

The third measure was the reversal of the termination of the Menominee Tribe by the Menominee Restoration Act of December 22, 1973, which Nixon declared was "an important turning point in the history of the American Indian people." By restoring the Menominees to federal trust status, he said, "the United States has at last made a clear reversal of a policy which was wrong, the policy of forcibly terminating Indian tribal status."[10]

These three laws were backed enthusiastically by Nixon and by the Indians and (in the context of the concern for Indian rights generated in large part by the Indian protest movement) garnered sufficient support in Congress for passage. They unmistakably signified the new status of Indian rights in the United States. A land claim of long standing had been validated, not merely by monetary compensation but by land itself; the principle of uninhibited access to religious sites had been recognized; and termination had been dealt a decisive blow. These all were examples of self-determination, since they acknowledged the wishes or demands of the Indians themselves.

One area in which the "new Indians" appeared in sharp light was that of legal action, taken to vindicate rights based on treaty guarantees or statute laws. Many of the suits brought by the Indians to recover lost land or to protect other rights were encouraged and supported by the Native American Rights Fund (NARF), a national legal defense organization founded in 1971. NARF assembled a group of young lawyers, two-thirds of them Indians, and used its funds to pursue cases and projects that would have a national impact. There has been what amounts to a judicial revolution in Indian affairs in our own time, as the courts have recognized Indian claims in diverse ways.

A highly successful maneuver resulted in Indian claims to land in the Atlantic Coast states—a region usually bypassed by federal Indian policy. Using a section of the 1790 trade and intercourse law that prohibited purchase of Indian land without the approval of the federal government, the Indians in Maine laid claim to millions of acres in the state, arguing that the land had been obtained illegally by Massachusetts (of which Maine was then a part) in violation of the 1790 law. The claim threw the state into economic turmoil, for it called in question thousands of land titles, and a negotiated settlement was reached in order to avoid a protracted legal battle. Indians in Massachusetts, Rhode Island, New York, and South Carolina have pursued similar claims.[11]

Fishing rights furnished another arena for court action, particularly in the state of Washington, where treaties with the tribes in the 1850s guaranteed the Indians "the right of taking fish, at all usual and accustomed grounds and stations . . . in common with all citizens of the Territory." In a notable decision in 1974, Judge George Boldt of the federal district court declared that those rights meant not only access to fishing sites but a fair share of the fish, which he ruled was up to fifty percent of the harvestable number of fish.[12] Similarly, Chippewa Indians, challenged by the state of Michigan for violating state fishing regulations, won in the federal courts, which, on the basis of aboriginal use and a treaty of 1836, denied the state the power to regulate Indian fishing.

The question of Indian water rights in the arid West also became a critical issue in the 1970s, for growing white population put increased pressure on limited water resources. As Indians sought to improve their economic condition, water for irrigation and for other uses became of supreme importance. The activism of the Indians in the 1970s was strongly reflected in strident demands that Indian water rights be protected, although no final quantification of Indian water rights was made.[13]

All these remarkable advances in Indian self-determination, however, did not touch directly a more universal principle enunciated by Nixon, namely, active participation of Indians in managing the education, health, and other social welfare programs supplied to them by the federal government, programs that vitally affected the everyday lives of all tribal members. Nixon's intention was stated in his 1970 message: "We have concluded that Indians will get better programs and that public monies will be more effectively expended if the people who are most affected by these programs are responsible for operating them." To this end the administration prepared a bill, which was introduced on April 19, 1971. The measure provided for the transfer to Indian tribes, at their own request, of federal programs and services, with the federal government furnishing the funds and technical assistance. It was known as a "takeover" bill, by which the Indians would assume full responsibility. "Only this approach," an Interior Department spokesman asserted, "squarely meets the Administration goal of Indian self-determination." The Department of Health, Education, and Welfare, which administered the massive Indian health programs, also urged its passage.[14]

But at this point the clear streams moving toward Indian autonomy and self-determination were seriously muddied by an oft-recurring, almost pervasive, phenomenon: Indian hesitation—or refusal—to set aside their dependency and to accept the responsibility offered.

The Indians opted for a substitute measure, by which Indian tribes would merely be parties to contracts negotiated with the appropriate department secretary (interior or HEW). The specific terms of each contract would determine the amount of Indian involvement in a given program. The responsibility would still rest with the federal agency, which could decide which contracts to approve, determine the limits of the contracts, and in general maintain control over the programs. William Youpee, president of the National Tribal Chairmen's Association, expressed an Indian consensus in favor of the limited contracting. As for the takeover bill, he said that "most of the reservations kind of feel this would maybe eventually lead to termination." Franklin Ducheneaux, speaking for the National Congress of American Indians, likewise rejected the administration bill, noting that it "may be the wave of the future" but that it had not received substantial support from Indians.[15]

The outcome was the Indian Self-Determination and Education Assistance Act of January 4, 1975, which in its preamble pointed to the tension between the competing philosophies. The United States recognized its obligation to respect "the strong expression of the Indian people for self-determination by assuring maximum Indian participation in the direction of educational as well as other Federal services to Indian communities so as to render such services more responsive to the needs and desires of these communities," while it also declared its commitment to maintaining "the Federal Government's unique and continuing relationship with and responsibility to the Indian people." The preamble spoke of providing "an orderly transition from federal domination to effective Indian participation in planning and administering programs."[16]

The results of the law were mixed. On the one hand Indian communities made considerable use of the law to assume—by contract—the administration of important educational and health-care programs. Thus in fiscal year 1980, 370 tribes contracted for the operation of 200 million dollars' worth of programs under the act, and $22.3 million was paid to the tribes to cover their overhead in the contracts. Yet Indian spokesmen noted that the federal departments still made basic decisions about the contracts, and they charged that use of this ultimate authority negated the effects intended by Congress in the legislation. Tribal leaders spoke of massive resistance to contracting by employees of the BIA—the "backlash of a paternalistic organization"—and insufficient technical assistance from the bureau as well as the increased burden of paperwork entailed by the contract procedure. The law, said the president of the National Tribal Chairmen's Association, was "an extraordinary example of the institutional power and capacity of some Federal Bureaucracies to preserve and protect themselves against the will of the people they serve." Thus representatives of the same organizations that had rejected legislation to allow tribes to assume full responsibility for programs and had instead supported the contracting scheme were now singing a different tune. There was also the fear, so often expressed, that contracting for programs was simply "concealed termination." [17]

The BIA's answer to the charges rested firmly on the ultimate responsibility of the federal officials. "The act does not relieve the Bureau of program responsibility," one spokesman noted. "Tribal assumption of program operation under contract is [only] another, a different, method for carrying out the Bureau's program responsibility." [18]

Here we are at the heart of the ongoing paradox. If the federal government retains responsibility (now increasingly called "trust responsibility") for Indian programs, it must maintain some control of them. But federal control negates full tribal self-determination.

The best theoretical manifestation of the paradox came in the work of the American Indian Policy Review Commission (AIPRC), authorized on January 2, 1975 (two days before the Indian Self-Determination Act). [19] The AIPRC was the brainchild of Senator James Abourezk of South Dakota, who wanted a careful study of the Indians' legal status which would be the basis for wiping out the current complexity and confusion in Indian policy. He saw it as a new Meriam Report with long-range objectives for corrective action, a blueprint for future Indian policy. The commission comprised eleven members—three senators, three representatives, and five Indians—and it was aided by eleven task forces (composed almost entirely of Indians), which investigated specific aspects of Indian affairs—health and education, for example—and the structure of federal administration of Indian affairs.

The commission accomplished very little, unfortunately, partly because of constraints of time and the lack of competent personnel, but in large part because it took an extreme advocacy position on the questions of Indian sovereignty and the federal trust responsibility. Its final report, submitted on May 17, 1977, asserted unequivocally, "Indian tribes are sovereign political bodies, having the power to determine their own membership and power to enact laws and enforce them within the boundaries of their reservations." But it also insisted on a broadened view of federal trust responsibility extending not only to protection of Indian resources but to the enhancement of tribal self-government and the provision of "economic and social programs necessary to raise the standard of living and social well being of the Indian people to a level comparable to the non-Indian society." It asserted that this trust responsibility extended to all Indians, whether on or off the reservation, and applied to all United States agencies, not just those charged specifically with the administration of Indian affairs. The AIPRC made 206 specific recommendations to carry out its principles. In spite of the strong assertion of Indian sovereignty, most of the recommendations began "Congress should appropriate money to . . . ."[20]

The conclusions of the commission were too much for the vice chairman, Representative Lloyd Meeds of Washington. In a vigorous dissenting statement, he blasted the report for being "one-sided advocacy" of the two controversial positions—inherent full sovereignty of the tribes and broad trust responsibilities of the federal government. He argued that the report sought to convert "a political notion into a legal doctrine."[21]

The reports of the AIPRC and its task forces now gather dust on office shelves, but the issues raised by the reports and by Meeds's dissent have persisted. They are fundamental questions in the determination of the legal status of the Indian tribes. Little by little they are being addressed and resolved—not by a single authoritative statement from some blue-ribbon commission, but piece by piece in court decisions, administrative regulations, and legislative enactments.

Crucial above all else is the question of the inherent sovereignty of the tribes. Do they have such sovereignty—independent of grants of authority from Congress—and what is its extent? The courts have adopted the doctrine of inherent tribal sovereignty set forth by Collier's associate, the lawyer Felix S. Cohen, in his famous *Handbook of Federal Indian Law,* published in 1942. Cohen wrote:

> Perhaps the most basic principle of all Indian law, supported by a host of decisions . . . is the principle that *those powers which are lawfully vested in an Indian tribes are not, in general, delegated powers granted by express acts of Congress, but rather inherent powers of a limited sovereignty which has never been extinguished.* Each Indian tribe begins its relationship with the Federal Government as a sovereign power, recognized as such in treaty and legislation. The powers of sovereignty have been limited from time to time by special

treaties and laws designed to take from the Indian tribes control of matters which, in the judgment of Congress, these tribes could no longer be safely permitted to handle. The statutes of Congress, then, must be examined to determine the limitations of tribal sovereignty rather than to determine its sources or its positive content. What is not expressly limited remains within the domain of tribal sovereignty.[22]

In 1978, in the case of *United States* v. *Wheeler*, the United States Supreme Court explicitly accepted this principle, but it also clearly pointed out its limitations. The court noted that before the coming of the Europeans, Indian tribes were indeed "self-governing sovereign political communities," which had "inherent power to prescribe laws for their members and to punish infractions of those laws." But the "full attributes of sovereignty" no longer remained. By treaties, by statutes, and by the exercise of Congress's "plenary control" over Indian affairs, elements of Indian sovereignty had been taken away. The court noted, however, that not all was gone, even though it insisted that what remained was of "a unique and limited character." Indian sovereignty exists, it said, "only at the sufferance of Congress and is subject to complete defeasance. But until Congress acts, the tribes retain their existing sovereign powers."[23]

This principle gives the Indians a whole lot, and it is truly remarkable. Indian tribes are composed of United States citizens, who nevertheless have a governmental power that antedates the United States and is in a sense separate from and independent of the sovereignty of the general government. The catch, of course, is that it exists only at the will of Congress and is subject to complete annulment if Congress should so act.

But Congress has not acted in many areas, and tribal

governments can exercise a good many powers of sovereignty. They can set up their own form of government, determine their own membership, administer justice to tribal members, tax, and regulate domestic relations and members' use of property. They can establish hunting and fishing regulations for their own members within the reservations and can zone and regulate land use. They can do a great many things that independent political entities do—insofar as federal law has not preempted their authority.

The most controverted question regarding inherent tribal sovereignty is the extent of tribal jurisdiction on the reservations. It is a difficulty compounded by the fact that within the reservation boundaries is a checkerboard of Indian property and white property that resulted from the allotment of Indian reservation lands under the Dawes Act of 1887. Whites purchased "surplus lands" not allotted to Indians and also many of the allotments once the Indians got a fee simple title to them that enabled them to sell. Tribes would like to exert jurisdiction over all the persons and all the property within the old boundaries; whites reject the notion of being subject to the tribal police and tribal courts.[24]

In 1978 the Supreme Court, in the case of *Oliphant* v. *Suquamish Indian Tribe*, made an important ruling in the matter. Mark Oliphant, a non-Indian residing on the Port Madison Reservation in the state of Washington, had been arrested by tribal authorities and charged with assaulting a tribal officer and resisting arrest. He claimed that he was not subject to tribal authority, and the Supreme Court upheld his claim. It declared: "Indian tribes do not have inherent jurisdiction to try and to punish non-Indians."[25]

Oliphant was taken by Indians as a damaging blow to their sovereign revival, a step backward in the progress made in recent years; it emphasized the fragile nature of tribal sovereignty and the ultimate power of the federal government in determining the extent and limitations of that sovereignty. The court, in fact, in 1981, restated the *Oliphant* doctrine in *Montana* v. *United States*, which concerned the right of the Crow Indian Tribe to regulate hunting and fishing of nonmembers on fee title lands held by non-Indians within the reservation. After noting inherent tribal power over tribal domestic concerns, the court said: "But exercise of tribal power beyond what is necessary to protect tribal self-government or to control internal relations is inconsistent with the dependent status of the tribes, and so cannot survive without express congressional delegation." It repeated bluntly "the general proposition" that "inherent sovereign powers of an Indian tribe do not extend to the activities of nonmembers of the tribe."[26]

Thus the courts are moving toward a clearer definition of tribal sovereignty. Retained inherent power is affirmed as it applies to tribal members; its application in given cases to nonmembers is denied. But new cases will undoubtedly arise to define still more explicitly tribal sovereignty and jurisdiction, for it remains a problem of crucial importance to Indian self-determination.

Still another indication of the movement toward self-determination was the Indian Child Welfare Act of 1978. The new law came in response to revelations of shocking statistics that showed the breaking up of Indian families by placement of Indian children in adoptive and foster homes among the white population. White social workers, under BIA and state programs, in a sincere effort to protect children of broken homes or otherwise unsatisfactory conditions had thoughtlessly promoted the involuntary separation of children from their parents that had marked the old boarding school experience. To reverse this practice, the new law provided for the jurisdiction of Indian tribes in child custody proceedings and the right of the tribe or Indian parents to intervene in state court proceedings. Moreover, it gave preference in adoptions first to the child's extended family, then to other members of the child's tribe, and finally to other Indian families. The act, in addition, authorized the establishment of child and family service programs on or near reservations to help prevent the breaking up of Indian families.[27]

Like other legislation, however, the Indian Child Welfare Act emitted mixed signals on the issue of self-determination. Although the law aimed to preserve Indian culture through stable Indian families and established tribal jurisdiction over Indian child custody cases, it on the other hand justified federal intervention in the matter on the grounds that "Congress has plenary power over Indian affairs." The grants for tribal child and family service programs were firmly in the hands of the Bureau of Indian Affairs, and the funds came from federal, not Indian, sources.

Meanwhile Indian tribes deal with the federal government under the vague principle today called government-to-government relations. President Ronald Reagan made use of the concept in his statement on Indian affairs of January 1983. He spoke of "a unique political relationship between Indian tribes and the United States which this administration pledges to uphold." "Our policy," he said, "is to reaffirm dealing with Indian tribes on a government-to-government basis and to pursue the policy of self-government for Indian tribes without threatening termination." The phrase also appears in the 1980 list of "Indian Tribal Entities That Have a Government-to-Government Relationship with the United States" printed in the *Federal Register*. In this context it takes on a different sense, however, for the heading to the list states simply: "The United States recognizes its trust responsibility to these Indian entities and, therefore, acknowledges their eligibility for programs administered by the Bureau of Indian Affairs."[28]

Here is another indication of the paradox. For many Indian communities the concept of "government-to-government" relations has little or no reference to inherent sovereignty or self-determination. The principle is simply an entitlement, a ticket, to the largess of federal Indian programs. It is the second element, in large part, that has made nonrecognized tribes seek federal acknowledgment.

The need for these federal programs and the attempt to transform them into a legal obligation through an expanded definition of trust responsibility points up a fundamental obstacle to the Indians' sovereignty and tribal autonomy. The Indian tribes and the reservations on which they are based are not economically self-sufficient. Dependency persists (and with it paternalism). No one wants it, but no one knows how to eliminate it.

None of the attempts to replace the self-sufficient economies of the aboriginal Indians with an economic base that will work in the twentieth century have succeeded. The nineteenth-century reformers were convinced that they had found the answer in the agriculture of the independent farmer. When they ultimately got Congress to enact their solution on a broad general basis in the Dawes Act (with its allotment of homestead-size farms to Indian families), they believed that the "end of the Indian problem" was in sight. By the 1920s the failure of allotment was apparent to all but its most adamant supporters, and John Collier ended the policy in 1934.

Collier's substitute was a return to communal tribal organization and tribal corporations to carry on business enterprise. But the Indians had almost as little success with this as they had had with individual allotments. In the first ten years of the Indian New Deal only seventy-three tribes organized the corporations that Collier promoted. The failure came in part because Collier misunderstood the Indians' traditional economic units; in large part, too, the reservations did not offer the economic means that were needed for self-sufficiency. Nor did the stimulus to the production and marketing of arts and crafts that Collier so strongly advocated furnish an answer.

Termination in the 1950s proved beyond much doubt that pushing even the most economically prosperous tribes into the marketplace on their own, freed of federal protection and support, would not work. And although migration of many Indians from the reservations to the cities relieved the pressure of overcrowding on the reservations, it did not increase the economic resources there and in a sense merely transferred many Indians from rural poverty to urban poverty.

Industrial development on the reservations, so eagerly promoted since the 1960s, did not take hold, for white entrepreneurs found the reservations unattractive. At oversight hearings in the House of Representatives in 1979 the assistant secretary of the interior for Indian affairs described the numerous positive programs of economic activity on the reservations, but he was forced to conclude: "Reservations lack some or all of the attributes necessary to support economic enterprise functions. Reservations have no tax base, often are bleak and barren, remote from labor pools, raw materials, and markets; transportation and power may be minimal or nonexistent."[29] The need was clearly recognized; the programs to meet it all seemed ineffective.

Meanwhile federal support of reservation life continued and indeed increased. Although the ultimate goal of federal spending was to assist the Indians to shake off their dependency and become self-supporting, Indian communities and individual Indians continued to need outside help to bring them up to the economic and social level of other American citizens. Programs for education, health, and social services; construction of schools, hospitals, and roads; irrigation systems and resource development all were provided from federal funds. Year by year the amounts grew, as more needs were recognized and as Indian demands for goods and services became stronger and better articulated.

The chief supplier of the programs was the Bureau of Indian Affairs in the Department of the Interior; its budget for 1980 totaled more than a billion dollars, of which education costs made up the largest share ($271,762,000). Added to that amount was another two billion dollars for services from other federal departments—including the education programs of the Department of Education and the Indian health services of the Department of Health and Human Services.[30] These were appropriations for strictly Indian programs; the Indians, as poverty-stricken groups, also drew heavily upon welfare programs available to all citizens.

The dependency that comes from such a situation is inescapable, and the programs of services, care, and relief do not of themselves advance reservation self-sufficiency. Commissioner of Indian Affairs William E. Hallett put his finger on the problem precisely in a 1980 report:

> During the past decade and a half, federal monies have gone to Indian communities in unprecedented amounts. Those dollars bought better education, health care, housing, public employment and roads. In some ways, at least, they resulted in a noticeable improvement in the quality of reservation life.
>
> What those dollars did not buy was substantive economic development. And if this trend continues, tribes may become overwhelmingly dependent upon direct and indirect government subsidies. That would be a tragedy for both the Indian people and the nation.[31]

As federal services became more deeply engrained in Indian existence, there was an increasing tendency to justify them under the broadened concept of trust responsibility. The National Tribal Chairmen's Association's response to President Reagan's Indian policy statement was an example:

> The federal government gained a territory in perpetuity over which to govern through treaties and other agreements with Indian nations, with promises to: 1) protect the Indians in their reserved territory and other private property, and 2) provide a variety of health, education and social services to Indian people, in perpetuity.
>
> The federal government historically has not lived up to its

trust responsibility to fulfill these promises, and it is for this
reason that the Indian people today suffer from the poorest
social and economic conditions of any population in the United
States.[32]

This same position has been repeated over and over
until many Indians and their advocates accept it as fact.
Yet the promises of education and other assistance made
in the land cession treaties and agreements were actually
for a limited time period only, for it was the general
belief that Indians would be absorbed into the dominant
society and would no longer need the services. Since that
did not happen, the federal government has continued
and increased the services because of its recognition of
the Indians' need, not on the basis of legal promises.

The Indian drive for self-determination and sovereignty, in many ways so fruitful and successful and, most
importantly, accepted as an official goal of the United
States, carries within it the contradictory seeds of dependency. Even the government's trust responsibility in regard to land and other Indian assets, which all agree are
legally incumbent upon the federal government, entail an
element of paternalism. As Interior Department officials
asserted in 1973,

> The exercise of a trust is paternalism. Indian leaders, govern-
> ment officials and the general public should understand that the
> Indian demands that the government continue its trust respon-
> sibility for Indian assets inescapably involve paternalism. The
> government has to approve proposed uses or disposition of the
> assets under its trust responsibility. To do otherwise is to
> violate the trust. If the Indians want to do otherwise—that is,
> have complete freedom for use of their assets—they should
> request legislation terminating the trust responsibility."[33]

When the trust responsibility is extended to include "health, education and social services to Indian people, in perpetuity," paternalism becomes almost unlimited in scope and in duration, for the federal government becomes the supplier of the Indians' essential needs. Dependence on the federal government for schooling, health care, legal services, technical aid in tribal government, and economic development means the nineteenth-century Great Father redivivus in pervasive form.

We have looked at two centuries of the history of Indians in American society from the Revolutionary War to the present day. The years were full of paradoxes and anomalies, yet patterns of paternalism and dependency were clear enough. The United States government, imbued with the humane ideals of the Enlightenment at its birth, deeply influenced by evangelical Christianity as it matured, and (when the idea of the "Christian nation" faded after 1920) accepting a genuine interest in the Indian people under social science culture concepts and an ideal of pluralism, showed a benevolent concern for its children or wards. Though the motivation changed, paternalism remained constant. The Indians always seemed to be in need, for the various reasons these essays have explored. The Indians were dependent for their well-being upon federal protection and largess. That much was owed them in return for the land of the continent they once occupied all by themselves does not lessen the fact—or the spirit—of dependency.

Assimilation would have ended all relationships of paternalism and dependency, as tribal entities disappeared and individual Indians merged completely into the dominant culture. But the policy of assimilation was tried and found wanting, although it still has its advocates. The alternative, self-sufficiency for Indian communities on which a degree of political and cultural autonomy can be based, has not yet reached fruition. Unless it does, or until it does, the American Indians will remain dependent on a paternalistic government.

Notes

1. Paternalism

1. Vine Deloria, Jr., *Custer Died for Your Sins: An Indian Manifesto* (New York: Macmillan Co., 1969), p. 28. The term *conquistador mentality* comes from Wilbur R. Jacobs, *Dispossessing the American Indian: Indians and Whites on the Colonial Frontier* (New York: Charles Scribner's Sons, 1972), pp. 23, 28, 30. A widely read example of the genre is Dee Brown, *Bury My Heart at Wounded Knee: An Indian History of the American West* (New York: Holt, Rinehart and Winston, 1971).

2. Edward Pessen, *Jacksonian America: Society, Personality, and Politics,* rev. ed. (Homewood, Illinois: Dorsey Press, 1978), pp. 296–297.

3. Comments of Roxanne Dunbar Ortiz on a paper given by Francis Jennings, "The Interaction of Historians and Anthropologists in the Writing of American Indian History" (Seventy-third Annual Meeting of the Organization of American Historians, San Francisco, April 10, 1980).

4. Michael Paul Rogin, *Fathers and Children: Andrew Jackson and the Subjugation of the American Indian* (New York: Alfred A. Knopf, 1975); quotations from pp. 9–11. For other psychohistorical approaches to Indian affairs, see Richard Slotkin, *Regeneration through Violence: The Mythology of the American Frontier, 1600–1860* (Middletown, Connecticut: Wesleyan University Press, 1973), and Richard Drinnon, *Facing West: The Metaphysics of Indian-Hating and Empire-Building* (Minneapolis: University of Minnesota Press, 1980).

5. Thomas Jefferson to Chastellux, June 7, 1785, *The Papers of Thomas Jefferson,* ed. Julian Boyd, 20 vols. to date (Princeton:

Princeton University Press, 1950——), 8:186; Jefferson, *Notes on the State of Virginia* (Richmond: J. W. Randolph, 1853), p. 67.

6. Thomas L. McKenney, *Memoirs, Official and Personal: With Sketches of Travels among the Northern and Southern Indians,* 2 vols. in 1 (New York: Paine and Burgess, 1846), 2:14–15. See also Herman J. Viola, *Thomas L. McKenney: Architect of America's Early Indian Policy, 1816–1830* (Chicago: Swallow Press, 1974).

7. Report of the Commissioner of Indian Affairs, 1868, in *House Executive Document* no. 1, 40th Congress, 3d session, serial 1366, p. 477; Thomas J. Morgan, "A Plea for the Papoose," in *Americanizing the American Indians: Writings by the "Friends of the Indian," 1880–1900,* ed. Francis Paul Prucha (Cambridge: Harvard University Press, 1973), pp. 241–242.

8. It is common today to emphasize the agricultural accomplishments of many Indian groups. White observers in the nineteenth century, of course, noted Indian farming, and early settlers often depended upon Indian crops for subsistence. But the Indians also depended upon hunting and gathering, and this fact was used to characterize Indian societies in general; hunter societies were taken to be inferior to agricultural societies. President Monroe, for example, asserted in 1817 that "the hunter or savage state requires a greater extent of territory to sustain it, than is compatible with the progress and just claims of civilized life, and must yield to it." He told Congress that "the earth was given to mankind to support the greatest number of which it is capable, and no tribe or people have a right to withhold from the wants of others more than is necessary for their own support and comfort." Monroe to Andrew Jackson, October 5, 1817, *Correspondence of Andrew Jackson,* ed. John Spencer Bassett, 6 vols. (Washington: Carnegie Institution of Washington, 1926–1933), 2:331; message of December 2, 1817, *The State of the Union Messages of the Presidents, 1790–1966,* ed. Fred L. Israel, 3 vols. (New York: Chelsea House, 1966), 1:152.

9. Jefferson to William Henry Harrison, February 27, 1803, *The Writings of Thomas Jefferson,* ed. Andrew A. Lipscomb, 20 vols. (Washington: Thomas Jefferson Memorial Association, 1903–1904), 10:370–371; Calhoun report of January 15, 1820, *American State Papers: Indian Affairs* 2:200–201.

10. Report of the Commissioner of Indian Affairs, 1844, in *Senate Document* no. 1, 28th Congress, 2d session, serial 449, p. 315;

Morgan, "A Plea for the Papoose," p. 241.

11. For the history of the theory of stages of society based on different modes of subsistence, see Ronald L. Meek, *Social Science and the Ignoble Savage* (Cambridge: Cambridge University Press, 1976). A classic account of the theory is Lewis Henry Morgan, *Ancient Society, or Researches in the Lines of Human Progress from Savagery through Barbarism to Civilization* (New York: Henry Holt and Co., 1877). A striking use of the theory by Thomas Jefferson is in Jefferson to William Ludlow, September 6, 1824, *Writings of Jefferson*, ed. Lipscomb, 16:74–75.

12. *The American Heritage Dictionary of the English Language*, s.v. *paternalism*; John W. Bennett, "Paternalism," in *International Encyclopedia of the Social Sciences*. I do not subscribe to the view that paternalism was projected on the Indians to satisfy unconscious needs of white society. See the extended discussion of paternalism in this light in Rogin, *Fathers and Children*.

13. Records of the Office of the Secretary of War, Indian Affairs, letters sent, vol. A, p. 143, Record Group 75, National Archives.

14. Message of January 18, 1803, *A Compilation of the Messages and Papers of the Presidents, 1789–1897*, comp. James D. Richardson, 10 vols. (Washington: Government Printing Office, 1896–1899), 1:352.

15. The humanitarian aspects of McKenney's work are discussed at length in Viola, *Thomas L. McKenney*.

16. McKenney to Eli Baldwin, October 28, 1829, Records of the Office of Indian Affairs, letters sent, vol. 6, p. 140, Record Group 75, National Archives. In a conversation with Jeremiah Evarts, the most outspoken opponent of Indian removal, McKenney said, "These questions of abstract right are of no use. The Cherokees are like children in a house on fire. We must pull them out." E. C. Tracy, *Memoir of the Life of Jeremiah Evarts, Esq.* (Boston: Crocker and Brewster, 1845), p. 360. McKenney's endeavors to promote Indian removal are discussed in Francis Paul Prucha, "Thomas L. McKenney and the New York Indian Board," *Mississippi Valley Historical Review* 48 (March 1962): 635–655.

17. *Cherokee Nation* v. *Georgia*, 5 Peters 17.

18. Jackson to James Gadsden, October 12, 1829, *Correspondence*, ed. Bassett, 4:81.

19. Message of February 15, 1832, *Messages and Papers*, comp.

Richardson, 2:566; Farewell Address, March 4, 1837, ibid., 3:294.

20. See the discussion in Francis Paul Prucha, *American Indian Policy in the Formative Years: The Indian Trade and Intercourse Acts, 1790–1834* (Cambridge: Harvard University Press, 1962), pp. 234–235, and in Francis Paul Prucha, *American Indian Policy in Crisis: Christian Reformers and the Indian, 1865–1900* (Norman: University of Oklahoma Press, 1976), pp. 63–70.

21. Francis A. Walker, *The Indian Question* (Boston: J. R. Osgood and Co., 1874), p. 8.

22. An example is the Oto and Missouri Treaty of March 15, 1854, printed in *Indian Affairs: Laws and Treaties,* comp. Charles J. Kappler, 5 vols. (Washington: Government Printing Office, 1904–1941), 2:608–611. See also the treaties with the tribes of the Pacific Northwest in 1854–1855, ibid., pp. 655–677, 682–685, 694–706; treaty with the Utes, August 8, 1855, ibid., 5:687.

23. "Records of the Proceedings of the Commission to Hold Treaties with the Indian Tribes in Washington Territory and the Blackfoot Country," Records of the Office of Indian Affairs, Documents Relating to the Negotiation of Ratified and Unratified Treaties with Various Indian Tribes, Record Group 75, National Archives (T494, reel 5, frames 206–209); Margaret Stevens letters, February 17 and 18, 1855, quoted in Kent D. Richards, *Isaac I. Stevens: Young Man in a Hurry* (Provo, Utah: Brigham Young University Press, 1979), p. 195.

24. *Army and Navy Journal* 5 (December 7, 1867); 251, citing "a correspondent of the Philadelphia *Press.*"

25. *Proceedings of the Great Peace Commission of 1867–1868* (Washington: Institute for the Development of Indian Law, 1975), pp. 86–87.

26. Ibid., p. 116.

27. See the treaties signed at Fort Laramie with the Sioux, Arapaho, Crow, and Cheyenne Indians in 1868, *Indian Affairs: Laws and Treaties,* comp. Kappler, 2:998–1015. Similar treaties were signed with the Navajos, Shoshonis, and Bannocks in the same year: ibid., pp. 1015–1024.

28. For the formation of the board and its composition see Prucha, *American Indian Policy in Crisis,* pp. 33–38.

29. *Annual Report of the Board of Indian Commissioners,* 1869, pp. 9–11.

30. See Prucha, *American Indian Policy in Crisis,* pp. 46–54.

31. Carl Schurz, "Present Aspects of the Indian Problem," *North American Review* 133 (July 1881):7–9.

32. The policies and programs of these reformers are treated in Prucha, *American Indian Policy in Crisis,* chaps. 5–12. Extensive selections from their writings are reprinted in Prucha, *Americanizing the American Indians*.

33. Report of the Commissioner of Indian Affairs, 1892, in *House Executive Document* no. 1, part 5, 52d Congress, 2d session, serial 3088, pp. 24–25.

34. Report of the Commissioner of Indian Affairs, 1901, in *House Document* no. 5, 57th Congress, 1st session, serial 4290, p. 4.

35. Report of the Commissioner of Indian Affairs, 1914, in *House Document* no. 1475, 63d Congress, 3d session, serial 6815, pp. 7–8.

36. Ibid., p. 4; emphasis added.

37. Payne to Sells, November 16, 1920, Records of the Office of the Secretary of the Interior, Central Classified File 5–6, General, Patents, Record Group 48, National Archives.

2. Dependency

1. Edward H. Spicer, *A Short History of the Indians of the United States* (New York: Van Nostrand Reinhold Co., 1969), pp. 11–16.

2. *Indian Affairs: Laws and Treaties,* comp. Kappler, 2:8–11 (Cherokee 1785), 25 (Creek 1790), 74 (Sac and Fox 1804), 225 (Ponca 1825), 311 (Choctaw 1830).

3. The trade and intercourse laws are discussed at length in Prucha, *American Indian Policy in the Formative Years*.

4. 5 Peters 17–18.

5. Population figures are from *Historical Statistics of the United States, Colonial Times to 1970,* Bicentennial Edition, 2 vols. (Washington: Bureau of the Census, 1975), 1:8. There are no accurate figures for Indian population in the nineteenth century.

6. Much attention has been paid in recent years to the effects of Old World pathogens on the Indians. See, for example, Alfred W. Crosby, Jr., *The Columbian Exchange: Biological and Cultural Consequences of 1492* (Westport, Connecticut: Greenwood Publishing Co., 1972); Wilbur R. Jacobs, "The Tip of the Iceberg: Pre-Colum-

bian Indian Demography and Some Implications for Revisionism," *William and Mary Quarterly*, 3d ser., 31 (January 1974): 123–132; and Henry F. Dobyns, *Their Number Become Thinned: Native American Population Dynamics in Eastern North America* (Knoxville: University of Tennessee Press, 1983), pp. 7–32.

7. 6 Peters 560–561.

8. Notable examples of this new approach to the history of Indian-white relations are William Cronon, *Changes in the Land: Indians, Colonists, and the Ecology of New England* (New York: Hill and Wang, 1983), and Richard White, *The Roots of Dependency: Subsistence, Environment, and Social Change among the Choctaws, Pawnees, and Navajos* (Lincoln: University of Nebraska Press, 1983).

9. See White, *Roots of Dependency*, p. 316.

10. These changes are discussed in detail in Cronon, *Changes in the Land*.

11. White, *Roots of Dependency*, p. 146; see the full discussion of the Choctaws, pp. 1–146.

12. An excellent brief description of the changes among the Sioux is Robert M. Utley, *The Last Days of the Sioux Nation* (New Haven: Yale University Press, 1963), pp. 6–39.

13. Quoted in White, *Roots of Dependency*, p. 79.

14. Francis Paul Prucha and Donald F. Carmony, eds., "A Memorandum of Lewis Cass: Concerning a System for the Regulation of Indian Affairs," *Wisconsin Magazine of History* 52 (Autumn 1968): 40–41; Report of Cass and Clark, *Senate Document* no. 72, 20th Congress, 2d session, serial 181, p. 29.

15. Alexis de Tocqueville, *Democracy in America*, ed. J. P. Mayer and Max Lerner, trans. George Lawrence (New York: Harper and Row, 1966), p. 296.

16. For the government trading houses (factory system) see Francis Paul Prucha, *The Great Father: The United States Government and the American Indians* (Lincoln: University of Nebraska Press, 1984), chap. 4. The quotation from Washington is in *Messages and Papers*, comp. Richardson, 1:141.

17. *Proceedings of the Great Peace Commission of 1867–1868*, pp. 89, 92–93.

18. Ibid., p. 64.

19. Report of the Secretary of War, 1877, in *House Executive*

Document no. 1, part 2, 45th Congress, 2d session, serial 1794, p. 630.

20. Henry B. Whipple, "The Indian System," *North American Review* 99 (October 1864): 450–451; Report of the Commissioner of Indian Affairs, 1869, in *House Executive Document* no. 1, part 3, 41st Congress, 2d session, serial 1414, p. 448.

21. *United States Statutes at Large* 16:566.

22. Ibid. 23:385.

23. *Senate Report* no. 708, 46th Congress, 2d session, serial 1899, pp. xvi–xviii.

24. Report of the Commissioner of Indian Affairs, 1882, in *House Executive Document* no. 1, part 5, 47th Congress, 2d session, serial 2100, p. 107.

25. *Senate Executive Document* no. 51, 51st Congress, 1st session, serial 2682, p. 50.

26. Margaret Mead, *The Changing Culture of an Indian Tribe* (New York: Columbia University Press, 1932), p. 27.

27. *Indian Affairs: Laws and Treaties,* comp. Kappler, 2:1000–1001.

28. The best example of this viewpoint is in Report of the Commissioner of Indian Affairs, 1868, in *House Executive Document* no. 1, 40th Congress, 3d session, serial 1366, pp. 476–479.

29. The history of the Dawes Act is treated in Prucha, *Great Father,* pp. 660–671.

30. Report of the Commissioner of Indian Affairs, 1901, in *House Document* no. 5, 57th Congress, 1st session, serial 4290, pp. 1, 3–4.

31. The drive to free "competent" Indians from federal protection and supervision is discussed in Prucha, *Great Father,* pp. 879–885. A more detailed study is Janet A. McDonnell, "The Disintegration of the Indian Estate: Indian Land Policy, 1913–1929" (Ph.D. dissertation, Marquette University, 1980).

32. *Annual Report of the Board of Indian Commissioners,* 1921, pp. 5–9.

33. Report of the Commissioner of Indian Affairs, 1900, in *House Document* no. 5, 56th Congress, 2d session, serial 4101, p. 432.

34. Records of the Bureau of Indian Affairs, Office File of Hervey B. Peairs, entry no. 722, Record Group 75, National Archives.

35. Report of the Commissioner of Indian Affairs, 1920, in *House*

Document no. 849, 66th Congress, 3d session, serial 7820, p. 157.

36. Erik H. Erikson, *Childhood and Society*, 2d ed. (New York: W. W. Norton and Co., 1963), p. 119.

3. Indian Rights

1. *1970 Census of Population*, vol. 1, *Characteristics of the Population*, part 1, section 1, table 48.

2. Report of the Commissioner of Indian Affairs, 1905, in *House Document* no. 5, 59th Congress, 1st session, serial 4959, pp. 1–12. The early stirrings of interest in Indian arts and crafts is discussed in Robert Fay Schrader, *The Indian Arts and Crafts Board: An Aspect of New Deal Indian Policy* (Albuquerque: University of New Mexico Press, 1983), pp. 3–21.

3. These changes are discussed in Robert T. Handy, *A Christian America: Protestant Hopes and Historical Realities* (New York: Oxford University Press, 1970), pp. 184–225. See also a similar account in Sydney E. Ahlstrom, *A Religious History of the American People* (New Haven: Yale University Press, 1972), pp. 895–917.

4. Collier's career as a reformer is well treated in Kenneth R. Philp, *John Collier's Crusade for Indian Reform, 1920–1954* (Tucson: University of Arizona Press, 1977), and Lawrence C. Kelly, *The Assault on Assimilation: John Collier and the Origins of Indian Policy Reform* (Albuquerque: University of New Mexico Press, 1983).

5. On the dance controversy see Prucha, *Great Father*, pp. 800–805, and the sources cited there.

6. Lewis Meriam et al., *The Problem of Indian Administration* (Baltimore: Johns Hopkins Press, 1928).

7. The Rhoads-Scattergood administration is treated in Prucha, *Great Father*, pp. 921–939.

8. For Collier's work as commissioner see Prucha, *Great Father*, pp. 940–1012, and Philp, *John Collier's Crusade*, pp. 113–213.

9. Collier outlined his principles in his *Indians of the Americas: The Long Hope* (New York: W. W. Norton and Co., 1947), chap. 14.

10. The act is printed in *United States Statutes at Large* 48:984–988.

11. *Indians at Work* 1 (July 1, 1934): 1–2.

12. For criticisms of Collier's work see Philp, *John Collier's Crusade*, pp. 237–244; Lawrence C. Kelly, "The Indian Reorganiza-

tion Act: The Dream and the Reality," *Pacific Historical Review* 44 (August 1975): 291–312; Lawrence C. Kelly, "John Collier and the Indian New Deal: An Assessment," in *Indian-White Relations: A Persistent Paradox,* ed. Jane F. Smith and Robert M. Kvasnicka (Washington: Howard University Press, 1976), pp. 227–241; and Graham D. Taylor, *The New Deal and American Indian Tribalism: The Administration of the Indian Reorganization Act, 1934–45* (Lincoln: University of Nebraska Press, 1980).

13. Deloria, *Custer Died for Your Sins,* p. 145. An example of criticism of tribal governmental organization is a statement of William A. Means, director of the International Indian Treaty Council, in *Indian Truth,* April 1983, p. 7. Means says: "Unfortunately, these tribal governments do not represent the majority of the Indian population. Rather, they are administrative authorities imposed by the government and managed by the Bureau of Indian Affairs." For a sharp exchange of views on the subject see the statements of Wilcomb E. Washburn and Joseph De La Cruz in the *New York Times* (op-ed page), July 20 and August 2, 1978.

14. *Annual Report of the Secretary of the Interior,* 1934, pp. 78–83.

15. There is a general discussion of termination in Prucha, *Great Father,* pp. 1013–1084.

16. Arthur V. Watkins, "Termination of Federal Supervision: The Removal of Restrictions over Indian Property and Person," *Annals of the American Academy of Political and Social Science* 311 (May 1957): 55.

17. House Concurrent Resolution no. 108, August 1, 1953, *United States Statutes at Large* 67:B132.

18. There is a discussion of relocation in Prucha, *Great Father,* pp. 1079–1084. See also Elaine M. Neils, *Reservation to City: Indian Migration and Federal Relocation,* Research Paper no.131 (Chicago: Department of Geography, University of Chicago, 1971).

19. For a general account of Indian affairs in the 1960s see Prucha, *Great Father,* pp. 1087–1110.

20. *A Program for Indian Citizens: A Summary Report* (Albuquerque: Commission on the Rights, Liberties, and Responsibilities of the American Indian, 1961). The final report of the commission was published as William A. Brophy and Sophie D. Aberle, *The Indian: America's Unfinished Business* (Norman: University of Oklahoma Press, 1966).

21. *Declaration of Indian Purpose* (Chicago: American Indian Chicago Conference, 1961). See also Nancy Oestreich Lurie, "The Voice of the American Indian: Report on the American Indian Chicago Conference," *Current Anthropology* 2 (December 1961): 478–500.

22. *Report to the Secretary of the Interior by the Task Force on Indian Affairs*, July 10, 1961.

23. For Indian participation in programs of the Office of Economic Opportunity see Prucha, *Great Father*, pp. 1093–1095; Alan L. Sorkin, *American Indians and Federal Aid* (Washington: Brookings Institution, 1971), pp. 165–199; and Sar A. Levitan, *The Great Society's Poor Law: A New Approach to Poverty* (Baltimore: Johns Hopkins Press, 1969), pp. 263–270.

24. Robert L. Bennett, "New Era for the American Indian," *Natural History* 76 (February 1967): 6–11; report submitted by Bennett to Henry M. Jackson, July 11, 1966, copy in Desk Files of Robert L. Bennett, 70A–2935, box 150, Washington National Records Center.

25. *Public Papers of the Presidents of the United States: Lyndon B. Johnson, 1968–69* (Washington: Government Printing Office, 1970), pp. 335–344.

26. For Indian fear of termination see Prucha, *Great Father*, pp. 1097–1098, 1099–1100. Bennett's statement is in Robert L. Bennett to the under secretary of the interior, April 25, 1969, in Desk Files of Robert L. Bennett, 70A-2935, Legislation, box 150.

27. The act is in *United States Statutes at Large* 82:73–92. The origins of the act are discussed in Donald L. Burnett, Jr., "An Historical Analysis of the 1968 'Indian Civil Rights' Act," *Harvard Journal of Legislation* 9 (May 1972): 557–626.

28. See Prucha, *Great Father*, pp. 1108–1110, and the sources cited there.

29. 436 *U.S. Reports* 49–83.

4. Self-Determination

1. For a survey of Indian affairs in the 1970s see Prucha, *Great Father*, pp. 1111–1208.

2. There is a biographical sketch of MacDonald by Peter Iverson in *American Indian Leaders: Studies in Diversity*, ed. R. David Edmunds (Lincoln: University of Nebraska Press, 1980), pp. 222–241.

3. Surveys of Indian activism in the 1960s are Stan Steiner, *The New Indians* (New York: Harper and Row, 1968); Alvin M. Josephy, Jr., *Red Power: The American Indians' Fight for Freedom* (New York: American Heritage Press, 1971); and Robert C. Day, "The Emergence of Activism as a Social Movement," in *Native Americans Today: Sociological Perspectives*, ed. Howard M. Bahr, Bruce A. Chadwick, and Robert C. Day (New York: Harper and Row, 1972), pp. 506–532.

4. Sympathetic accounts of Alcatraz are Peter Blue Cloud, ed., *Alcatraz Is Not an Island* (Berkeley, California: Wingbow Press, 1972), and Richard Oakes, "Alcatraz Is Not an Island," *Ramparts* 11 (December 1972): 35–41.

5. Accounts of the BIA seizure are Robert Burnette and John Koster, *The Road to Wounded Knee* (New York: Bantam Books, 1974), pp. 195–219, and Vine Deloria, Jr., *Behind the Trail of Broken Treaties: An Indian Declaration of Independence* (New York: Delacorte Press, 1974), pp. 43–62.

6. See Burnette and Koster, *Road to Wounded Knee*, pp. 220–254; Deloria, *Behind the Trail of Broken Treaties*, pp. 62–83; and Clyde D. Dollar, "The Second Tragedy at Wounded Knee: A 1970s Confrontation and Its Historical Roots," *American West* 10 (September 1973): 4–11, 58–61.

7. Statement of Richard Nixon, September 27, 1968, printed in *Indian Record*, January 1969, pp. 1–2; *Public Papers of the Presidents of the United States: Richard Nixon, 1970* (Washington: Government Printing Office, 1971), pp. 564–576.

8. *United States Statutes at Large* 84:1437–1439; *Public Papers of the Presidents: Nixon, 1970*, pp. 1131–1132; Dabney Otis Collins, "Battle for Blue Lake: The Taos Indians Finally Regain Their Sacred Land," *American West* 8 (September 1971): 32–37.

9. *United States Statutes at Large* 84:688–716; D'Arcy McNickle, *Native American Tribalism: Indian Survivals and Renewals* (New York: Oxford University Press, 1973), pp. 158–159. The best general account of claims of the Alaska Natives is Rob-

ert D. Arnold, *Alaska Native Land Claims* (Anchorage: Alaska Native Foundation, 1976).

10. *United States Statutes at Large* 87:770–773; *Public Papers of the Presidents: Nixon, 1973,* p. 1023. For a full account of the restoration see Nicholas C. Peroff, *Menominee Drums: Tribal Termination and Restoration, 1954–1974* (Norman: University of Oklahoma Press, 1982).

11. A general article is Tim Vollman, "A Survey of Eastern Indian Land Claims, 1970–1979," *Maine Law Review* 31, no. 1 (1979): 5–16. The Maine Indian Claims Settlement Act, October 10, 1980, is in *United States Statutes at Large* 94:1785–1797.

12. Useful accounts of the fishing controversy in Washington are *Uncommon Controversy: Fishing Rights of the Muckleshoot, Puyallup, and Nisqually Indians,* Report Prepared for the American Friends Service Committee (Seattle: University of Washington Press, 1970); and *Indian Tribes: A Continuing Quest for Survival,* Report of the United States Commission on Civil Rights, June 1981, pp. 61–100.

13. The problem of water rights is explained in detail in Norris Hundley, Jr., "The Dark and Bloody Ground of Indian Water Rights: Confusion Elevated to Principle," *Western Historical Quarterly* 9 (October 1978): 455–482.

14. See the general discussion of this matter in Prucha, *Great Father,* pp. 1157–1162, and the sources cited there.

15. Ibid., p. 1159.

16. *United States Statutes at Large* 88:2203–2217.

17. The reaction to the law is discussed in Prucha, *Great Father,* pp. 1160–1162.

18. Ibid., p. 1161.

19. *United States Statutes at Large* 88:1910–1914.

20. American Indian Policy Review Commission, *Final Report* (Washington: Government Printing Office, 1977).

21. Meeds's statement is printed ibid., pp. 571–612.

22. Felix S. Cohen, *Handbook of Federal Indian Law* (Washington: Government Printing Office, 1942), p. 122.

23. 435 *U.S. Reports* 313–332.

24. Brief surveys of this complex issue are Arthur Lazarus, Jr., "Tribal Sovereignty under United States Law," in *Indian Sovereignty: Proceedings of the Second Annual Conference on Problems Concern-*

ing American Indians Today, ed. William R. Swagerty (Chicago: Newberry Library, 1979), pp. 28–46; and John Niemisto, "The Legal Powers of Indian Tribal Governments," *Wisconsin Academy Review* 28 (March 1982): 7–11.

25. 435 *U.S. Reports* 191–212. For criticism of the decision see Russel Lawrence Barsh and James Youngblood Henderson, "The Betrayal: *Oliphant* v. *Suquamish Indian Tribe* and the Hunting of the Snark," *Minnesota Law Review* 63 (April 1978): 609–640.

26. 450 *U.S. Reports* 544–581.

27. For the problem see Steven Unger, ed., *The Destruction of American Indian Families* (New York: Association on American Indian Affairs, 1977). The law is in *United States Statutes at Large* 92:3069–3073. See also Manuel P. Guerrero, "Indian Child Welfare Act of 1978: A Response to the Threat to Indian Culture Caused by Foster and Adoptive Placements of Indian Children," *American Indian Law Review* 7, no. 1 (1979): 51–77.

28. "Indian Policy," *Weekly Compilation of Presidential Documents* 19 (January 31, 1983): 98–99; *Federal Register* 45:27828–27830 (April 24, 1980).

29. "Indian Economic Development Programs," *Oversight Hearings before the Committee on Interior and Insular Affairs, House of Representatives, 96th Congress, 1st Session* (1979), pp. 115–126.

30. Funding for federal Indian programs in 1980 is reported in *Hearings before a Subcommittee of the Committee on Appropriations, House of Representatives, 97th Congress, 1st Session, Subcommittee on the Department of the Interior and Related Agencies* (1981), part 9, pp. 1279–1280.

31. *BIA Profile: The Bureau of Indian Affairs and American Indians* (Washington: Government Printing Office, 1981), p. 6.

32. Printed in *Indian Truth,* April 1983, p. 6.

33. Quoted in American Indian Policy Review Commission, Task Force One, *Report on Trust Responsibilities and the Federal-Indian Relationship, Including Treaty Review* (Washington: Government Printing Office, 1976), p. 49.

Index